A SWING THROUGH TIME

Golf in Scotland
1457-1743

OLIVE M. GEDDES

THE NATIONAL LIBRARY OF SCOTLAND

EDINBURGH : HMSO

INSIDE FRONT AND BACK COVERS:

*The Adam Wood Clubs courtesy of Royal Troon Golf Club.
The clubs comprise two irons (a heavy spur toe iron and a
square toe driving or light iron), and six woods. The woods have
been dated to the first quarter of the 18th century, while the irons
are pre-1700.*

*The illustrations of 17th-century Dutch tiles featured throughout
and the Dutch golf club heads on page 18 appear courtesy of
Archie Baird; the 18th-century golf club on page 38, courtesy of
the British Golf Museum, St Andrews; the featherie golf balls on
the introduction page and pages 26 and 30, courtesy of the
National Museums of Scotland; and the early 18th-century iron
club on page 38, courtesy of Sotheby's.*

British Library Cataloguing in Publication Data.

A catalogue record for this book is available from the British Library.

HMSO publications are available from:

HMSO Bookshops
71 Lothian Road, Edinburgh, EH3 9AZ
031-228 4181 Fax 031-229 2734
49 High Holborn, London, WC1V 6HB
071-873 0011 Fax 071-873 8200 (counter service only)
258 Broad Street, Birmingham, B1 2HE
021-643 3740 Fax 021-643 6510
Southey House, 33 Wine Street, Bristol, BS1 2BQ
0272 264306 Fax 0272 294515
9-21 Princess Street, Manchester, M60 8AS
061-834 7201 Fax 061-833 0634
16 Arthur Street, Belfast, BT1 4GD
0232 238451 Fax 0232 235401

HMSO Publications Centre
(Mail, fax and telephone orders only)
PO Box 276, London, SW8 5DT
Telephone orders 071-873 9090
General enquiries 071-873 0011
(queuing system in operation for both numbers)
Fax orders 071-873 8200

HMSO's Accredited Agents
(see Yellow Pages)
and through good booksellers

ISBN 0 11 494209 9

FOREWORD

A Swing Through Time is a welcome addition to golfing literature for me because it provides superb illustrations of the earliest written evidence for the game of golf in Scotland.

This is the 'prehistory' of golf covering the years before the formation of the earliest Clubs in the middle of the 18th century, a period often treated in only the sketchiest of detail in the standard works on golfing history. In this book the unique documentary history of the game is made available, and the full-colour illustrations are accompanied by transcripts of the texts. Early golfing equipment is also featured, and the pictorial evidence both from Britain and the Low Countries considered.

I congratulate the National Library of Scotland on its contribution to golfing history. This is a book that will appeal to all golfing enthusiasts from the ardent collector of memorabilia to the casual player. I commend it to you!

Ben Crenshaw

CONTENTS

ACKNOWLEDGEMENTS

In writing this book, I have had much helpful advice and information from a number of colleagues and golfing authorities. Peter Lewis, Director of the British Golf Museum, St Andrews, has been supportive throughout. Robert Gowland of Phillips, Chester, provided valuable information on early golfing equipment. Archie Baird of Gullane Golf Museum has given generously of his wealth of information on golfing history, and David Black has made many helpful suggestions. I would also like to thank my colleagues in the National Library of Scotland, particularly the staff of the Manuscripts Department, for their patience and forbearance, Kenneth Gibson of the Publications Division for his help and support, also Margaret Wilkes and Ian Anderson. For photography, grateful thanks are due to Steve MacAvoy of the Library and Marius Alexander.

My thanks also go to all the private individuals and institutions who have allowed me to reproduce photographs of their documents, golfing equipment, and paintings: their names are to be found in the captions.

INTRODUCTION

The origins of golf are a matter of mystery and controversy. Little, if any, evidence of the game in the form of golfing equipment or recognisable visual images survives from earlier than the mid-18th century. And so, for the 'Dark Ages' of golf — before the formalisation of the game with the establishment of the first Golfing Societies and Clubs — it is to written sources that we must turn for reliable information.

This book takes a close look at the earliest written records of the game in Scotland, from the 1457 Act of Parliament banning golf to the first printed book devoted entirely to the game — Thomas Mathison's poem, *The Goff*, published in 1743. The original documents and books, many from the collections of the National Library of Scotland, are reproduced, while transcripts, commentary, and interpretation of the sources illuminate not only the early days of golf, but also the society which gave rise to the world's most internationally popular game.

1 GOLF

THE 'UNPROFFITABLE' SPORT, 1457-91

Edinburgh, 6 March 1457. *Item it is ordanyt and decretyt ... [th]at ye futbawe and ye golf be uterly cryt done and not usyt and [th]at ye bowe markes be maid at all parochkirkes apair of buttes and schuting be usyt ilk sunday...*

Edinburgh, 6 March 1457. Item, it is ordained and decreed ... that football and golf be utterly condemned and stopped and that a pair of targets be made at all parish kirks and shooting be practised each Sunday.

FACING PAGE
Act of the Parliament of Scotland, 6 March 1457. James II's well-known decree of 1457 banned both football and golf. This is the first known written reference to the game of golf in Scotland. *Scottish Record Office, PA5/6.*

Scotland in the 15th century was a country in turmoil, plagued by a succession of child-kings, an over-mighty and ambitious nobility, and the recurring threat of invasion from a powerful southern neighbour. Throughout the century the Scottish kings struggled to assert their authority. In the early years James I sought to quell internal divisions and at the same time maintain an army strong enough to repel invaders by his policy of a *'firm and sure peace'*. In this climate military training was of the utmost importance, and archery practice was made compulsory for all males over twelve years of age.

It is against this background that the development of the peaceable game of golf we know today must be set, and it is from this period that the earliest known written references to the game come — references which show that, like all new games, golf met with the disapproval of the establishment.

The earliest known written reference to golf in Scotland dates from 1457, when Parliament decreed that *'ye fut bawe and ye golf be uterly cryt done and not usyt'*. Instead, the people were to practise their archery. This suggests that both golf and football were popular with the common people, if not with the authorities in 15th-century Scotland. Clearly, the official view was that the two games were a nuisance as well as a distraction from the practice of archery.

The 1457 Act does not specify where golf was being played, but if it was in enclosed spaces such as church yards and streets, as many golfing historians have surmised, the potential hazards can easily be imagined. As far as archery was concerned, however, there seem to have been few qualms about public safety. On the contrary, the 1457 Act reveals that target practice in the kirk yard was mandatory, and every man was to fire at least six shots at the targets set up there. Failure to do so meant a fine of two pennies, the money raised to be spent on drink to reward those who had complied with the Act.

The ban was repeated in 1471 when Parliament announced *'it is thocht expedient [th]at ... ye futbal and golf be abusit in tym cumyng and ye buttes maid up and schot usit eftir ye tenor of ye act of parlyament'*.[1] Similarly, in 1491, *'it is Statut and ordinit ... that in na place of the realme be usit fut bawis gouff or uthir sic unproffitable sports, but for common gude and defence of the realme be hantit*

[1] 'It is thought necessary that football and golf be abandoned in future and that butts should be made up and archery practised according to the meaning of the Act of Parliament.'

1

bowis schuting and markes before ordinit'.[2] James IV attempted to enforce this stern edict by imposing a collective penalty on the parish for each defiance.

In an earlier decree of 1424, the Scottish Parliament had banned football — it is *'statut and the king forbids that na man play at the fut ball under payne of liiid [i.e. four pence]'* — but had made no mention of golf. This may have been an accidental omission: James I had recently returned from eighteen years of captivity in England and the Act largely reiterates an English decree of 1363 banning football. It could, however, indicate that a significant rise in the popularity of golf in Scotland had occurred sometime during the second quarter of the 15th century.

It has now been established that golf, or certainly a variant of it, was being played in Europe before the game became so popular in Scotland that it was

Act of Parliament of Scotland, 6 May 1471. Scottish Record Office, PA/2/1.

banned by Parliament. Little is known of the nature of medieval games: the Scottish Acts of Parliament may indicate that a game known as golf was being played, but they give no indication as to how it was played.

There appears to have been a number of ball and stick games played from the Middle Ages if not earlier. Some of these games seem to have taken place in an enclosed and defined area, and others were played in more open spaces. Some involved aiming at a target above ground, while in other cases the object was to hit the ball into a hole. These games must have constantly changed and evolved from one another over the years.

Act of Parliament of Scotland, 18 May 1491. Scottish Record Office, PA/2/5.

---

[2]   'It is Statute and ordained ... that in no part of the country should football, golf, or other such pointless sports be practised, but for the common good and for the defence of the country archery should be practised and targets made up as previously ordained.'

Bede's 'Life of St Cuthbert', 12th century. In this illustration in a 12th-century manuscript of Bede's Life of St Cuthbert, at least two ball games are taking place and a stick is clearly visible. *Bodleian Library, University College MS. 165.*

Bede's Life of St Cuthbert, written towards the end of the 7th century, includes an intriguing passage on the boyhood pastimes of the young Cuthbert who grew up in the south of Scotland. *'There were one day some customary games going on in a field, and a large number of boys got together, amongst whom was Cuthbert, and in the excitement of boyish whims, several of them began to bend their bodies in various unnatural forms.'* No mention is made here of ball and stick games, but in an illustration relating to this specific passage in a 12th-century manuscript of Bede's Life there are at least two ball games taking place and a stick is clearly visible.[3] So, to the 12th-century mind, *'customary games'* included balls and sticks.

Decrees issued by the English Parliament from 1363 to 1409 promoting archery practice and banning distracting sports cite football as the main culprit: golf is not mentioned. There is a stained-glass window of about 1350 in Gloucester Cathedral depicting a boy playing with a club, but it can only be claimed from this that he is playing a golf-like game, and golf seems not to have reached England until the early 16th century.

Legend has it that 'colf', 'a golf-like game', was played at Loenen aan de Vecht in the Province of North Holland in the Low Countries as early as 1297, and decrees restricting and even prohibiting 'colf' provide documentary

---

[3]   Bodleian Library, University College MS. 165.

evidence that the game was played there from the 14th century. In Brussels, the magistrates issued an ordinance banning '*who ever plays ball with a club*' in 1360, and in 1387 Albrecht of Bavaria's charter to the city of Brielle forbade gambling with four exceptions, one of which was playing '*the ball with the club without the fortifications of our afor said city*'.[4]

Although there were no hard-and-fast rules at this time, it seems the game played in the Low Countries was not the same as that known in Scotland. Generally, 'colf' was about aiming at above-the-ground targets, while in Scotland golf meant aiming at holes in the ground. Dutch 'colf' was often played on ice within a defined area, while the Scottish game was more wide-ranging and does not appear to have kept to a pre-defined course. Generally, the Dutch played a 'short-game', while the Scots version was a 'long-game'.

It was not only the political authorities who disapproved of golf, but also the Church. While little documentation survives to throw light on the attitude of the pre-reformation Church in Scotland towards golf, the reformed Kirk clearly disapproved when it involved Sabbath-breaking. From about 1580 declarations to this effect were made by Kirk Sessions as far afield as Edinburgh, Perth, St Andrews, Leith, Banff, Cullen, and Stirling.

The South Leith Kirk Session records of 16 February 1610 note '*The said day it wes concludit be the haill Sessioune, that thair sallbe na public playing suffred on the Sabbath dayes As playing at the valley bowles, at the peney stane, archerie, gowfe ... And igif any beis fund playing publicklie in ane Zaird or in the feildis upon ane Sabbath day fra morne till even That they sall pay xxs to the pure, and also make their publik repentance before the pulpite*'.[5]

The Golf Book, c. 1500. The margin of this Flemish Book of Hours shows four figures playing with clubs and what appear to be balls of wood and leather. One of the figures is kneeling to play his shot.
British Library, Add MS.24098.

4   Steven J.H. van Hengel, *Early Golf* (Liechtenstein, 1982), pp. 17-19.
5   Cited by D. Robertson, *The South Leith Records* (Edinburgh, 1911), p. 8. 'The said day it was concluded by the whole Session, that there shall be no public playing permitted on the Sabbath days such as playing at bowls, at the penny stone, archery, golf...And if any found playing publicly in a yard or in the fields upon a Sabbath day from morning until evening they shall pay 20 shillings to the poor, and also make their public repentance before the pulpit.'

J.C. Dolman, 'The Sabbath Breakers', late 19th century. These two golfers appear unpleasantly surprised to be found golfing on the links by a pair of rather stern looking clerics.
Luffness New Golf Club.

In Humbie in East Lothian, *'James Rodger, Johne Rodger, Johne Howdan, Andrew Howdan, and George Patersone, were complained upon for playing at the golf upon ane Lord's Day'*, in 1651. The next day they *'were ordained to mak their public repentance ... [and] Johne Howdan was deposed from his office being ane deacon'*.[6]

The Kirk did not always disapprove of Sunday golf as such: its concern was sometimes only with those who indulged *'in tyme of sermonis'* and so were absent from church services. In the East Lothian parish of Tyninghame in the mid-17th century a group of masons called before the Kirk Session for *'playing at ze golf...in tyme of preiching at efternoone'* offered in their defence that *'thre preiching was ather done or neir endit befor they went to the lynkis'*. After promising not to repeat the offence they were merely admonished.[7]

In St Andrews, the Kirk Session penalised a number of offenders who played golf *'in tyme of fast and precheing, aganis the ordinances of the kirk'* and in 1599 it issued a fixed tariff of penalties. For a first offence there was a fine of 10 shillings; this rose to 20 shillings for a second offence; and *'for the third fault publick repentance, and the fourt fault depravation fra their offices'*.[8]

6   John Kerr, *The Golf Book of East Lothian* (Edinburgh, 1896), p. 38.
7   Kerr, p. 37.
8   H.S.C. Everard, *A History of the Royal and Ancient Golf Club, St Andrews, from 1754-1900* (London, 1907), pp. 33-4.

Despite the Church's attitude to golf, some clergymen were golfers themselves.. In his *Historie of the Kirk in Scotland* John Row tells of the ordeal of the Bishop of Galloway who, while playing golf on Leith Links in 1619, saw a vision of two men attacking him. Taking this as an indication of his wrong-doing in accepting the office of Bishop which he himself had previously decried, he is said to have thrown down his golf clubs, taken to his bed, and died.[9]

Golf balls are listed among the personal possessions of a number of Edinburgh merchants in the late 16th century.[10] These men were some of the most prominent of Edinburgh's citizens and their testaments indicate the spread and appeal of the game. Also in the 1590s, the Town Council, of which these same merchants may well have been members, objected to the defamation of the Sabbath by golfers. In 1592 the Edinburgh magistrates issued a proclamation banning games on Sundays, backing up that of the Kirk Session.[11] The fact that the Council found it necessary to add that the ban extended to its female citizens indicates that women too were enjoying the game.

> *Seing the Sabboth day being the Lords day, it becumis everie Cristiane to dedicate himselff, his houshald, and famelie to the service and worschip of God...na inhabitants of the samyn [burgh] be themselffis thair childrein, servands or fameleis be sene at ony pastymes or gammis within or without the town upoun the Sabboth day, sic as golf, archerie, rowbowlilis [i.e. row bowls], penny stane, kaitchpullis [i.e. hand tennis] or sic other pastymes...and als that thair dochters and wemen servands be nocht fund playing at the ball nor singing of profane sangs upoun the sam day, under sic paynes as the magestratts sall lay to thair chairge.*

As with the parliamentary edicts, the Town Councils found it necessary periodically to repeat their threats of imprisonment and fines for those who failed to conform. In Edinburgh this happened the following year, in 1593, when it was declared that '*dyvers inhabitants of this burgh repaires upoun the Sabboth day to the toun of Leyth and in tyme of sermonis are sene vagand athort the streitts, drynking in tavernis, or other wayis at golf, aircherie, or other pastymes upoun the Lynks, thairby profaning the Sabboth day*'.[12] Considerable fines were threatened for persistent defaulters. The earlier declaration had forbidden golf '*within or without the town*', suggesting that it was expected that there might be those who

---

[9]   John Row, *Historie of the Kirk in Scotland*, Maitland Club (Glasgow, 1842), pp. 81, 477.
[10] Margaret Sanderson, 'Edinburgh Merchants in Society, 1570-1603', in *The Renaissance and Reformation in Scotland*, edited by Ian B. Cowan and Duncan Shaw (Edinburgh, 1983), p. 197.
[11] *Extracts from the Records of the Burgh of Edinburgh, 1589-1603*, Scottish Burgh Record Society (London, 1927), p. 63.
[12] *Extracts from the Records of the Burgh of Edinburgh, 1589-1603*, Scottish Burgh Record Society (London, 1927), p. 86. 'Several inhabitants of this burgh repair on the Sabbath day to the town of Leith and at times of sermons are seen wandering around the streets, drinking in taverns, or otherwise at golf, archery, or other pastimes upon the Links, thereby profaning the Sabbath day.'

Detail from John Ainslie's 'Plan of Edinburgh and Leith', 1804. Here, Leith Links are described as *'A common for playing at the golf'*. Nearby, on the shore of the Firth of Forth, are *'Leith Sands or Race Ground'*. National Library of Scotland, EMS.s.365.

would attempt to avoid the ban by leaving town, and by the 1593 edict, which specifically mentions Leith, it seems this did indeed happen.

Links are the area of open, common land along the coastal strip, which form a feature of many Scottish towns, particularly on the eastern side of the country. In the late 16th century, and for many years to come, they offered poor grazing and were also used for military purposes and recreation. They were in effect the people's play ground. The days of grazing cattle and drilling soldiers might have long gone, but Scotland's links golf courses are renowned throughout the world.

Leith, Edinburgh's port, lay a few miles outside the capital in the late 16th century. In this town, apparently because of the lax attitude of the authorities, their Links were also used for recreation by the citizens of nearby Edinburgh. Leith's open, sandy links, an obvious venue for sportsmen, were used for archery and horse-racing as well as golf.

In addition to meeting with the disapproval of Parliament, the Kirk Sessions, and the Town Councils, golf also fell foul of the tradesmen's Guilds or Incorporations. In 1690, an Elgin silversmith, Walter Hay, was fined and reprimanded for selling wine outside the church, and *'playing at ye Boulis and Golffe upoane Sundaye'*.

The number of declarations forbidding golf, and their geographical spread throughout Scotland, give some indication of the game's popularity and of the reaction of those in authority to a recreation which in succeeding centuries was to become one of Scotland's great sports. That it was necessary in Scotland to ban golf by Act of Parliament in 1457, and then to repeat the ban in 1471 and 1491 on such an *'unproffitable sport'*, suggests that even the combined efforts of Parliament, the Town Councils, the Kirk Sessions, and the Guilds, were not entirely successful in suppressing the game.

2 THE ROYAL GAME
1502-1682

WHILE THE SCOTTISH KINGS HAD PREVIOUSLY RATIFIED ACTS WHICH FORBADE their subjects to play golf, by at least the early 16th century they had no inhibitions about playing the game themselves.

There may well have been political reasons for this change in attitude. James IV came to the throne in 1488 at the age of fifteen. By 1502 he had made a peace treaty with the English king, Henry VII, and in 1503 he married Henry's daughter, Margaret, at Holyrood Abbey in Edinburgh. Peace with England seems to have resulted in military training being considered less essential, and consequently games and pastimes became more acceptable.

Evidence that the Scottish kings played golf is provided by the Accounts kept by David Beaton of Creich, Lord High Treasurer of Scotland. Expenses for the minutiae of domestic life in the royal household appear, and James's varied interests are well represented: included are payments for books, equipment for the King's chemical experiments, entertainments for the court, as well as for outdoor pursuits such as golf, hunting, archery, horse-racing, bowls, and tennis.

James IV spent the month of February 1503 entirely in Edinburgh, and as the illustration from the Lord High Treasurer's Accounts shows, he

Accounts of the Lord High Treasurer for Scotland, February, 1503.
Payments for golfing equipment and probably a wager on a match were made for James IV in 1503.
Scottish Record Office, E21/6.

purchased golf clubs and balls on the 6th of that month. The three French crowns the King spent on 3 February, '*to play at the golf with the Earl of Bothwell*', almost certainly suggest they had a wager on the match and that the King lost. There is no indication as to where in Edinburgh they played or how they played.

The King's games of golf in Edinburgh were clearly not isolated incidents, as the Treasurer's Accounts also note expenditure on golf in Perth in 1502, and in 1506, at which time James was probably in St Andrews. The 1506 entry is of added interest for the relative cost of golf balls and clubs at the time. The clubs bought for the King cost one shilling each while the balls were three for a shilling.

Credit for introducing golf to England may well be due to James IV and his court following his marriage to Princess Margaret in 1503, as the game seems to have been known in England by 1513. In that year, Henry VIII's Queen, Katharine of Aragon, wrote in a letter to Cardinal Wolsey that '*all... [the King's] subjects be very glad, I thank God, to be busy at the golf*'.[1]

James IV's successors on the Scottish throne were also golfers. His son, James V, is believed to have played at Gosford in East Lothian, and legend has it that Mary, Queen of Scots, played at St Andrews as depicted in this Edwardian illustration. Unfortunately, there is no firm documentary evidence to show that Mary was among the first lady golfers, and the Lord High Treasurer's Accounts for her reign omit any reference to purchases of golf balls and clubs.

What has survived, however, are claims by Mary's enemies that she failed to behave as a royal widow should after the murder of her second husband, Lord Darnley, at Kirk o' Fields in February 1567. One of the misdemeanours referred to was her alleged indulgence in a game of golf in the grounds of Seton Palace in East Lothian within a few days of Darnley's death.

King James V is said to have been fond of Gosford, and... it was suspected by his contemporaries, that, in his frequent excursions to that part of the country, he had other purposes in view besides golfing and archery. Three favourite ladies, Sandilands, Weir and Oliphant, one of whom resided at Gosford and the others in the neighbourhood, were often visited by their Royal and gallant admirer.[2]

Mary, Queen of Scots, on the Links at St Andrews. Tradition has it that Mary, Queen of Scots, played golf on the Links at St Andrews. *Illustrated London News, 1905. National Library of Scotland.*

[1] Robert Browning, *A History of Golf* (London, 1955), p. 2.
[2] Neil Roy 'Topographical Description of the Parish of Aberlady', in *Transactions of the Society of Antiquaries of Scotland*, 1872, pp. 517-18.

Alexander Keirincx, 'Seton Palace and the Forth Estuary', c.1635-40.
Seton Palace in East Lothian where Mary, Queen of Scots, is said to have played golf with the Earl of Bothwell shortly after the death of her husband, Lord Darnley, in suspicious circumstances in 1567. The remains of the Palace were demolished in 1789 to make way for the present Adam house.
Scottish National Portrait Gallery.

In his *Rerum Scoticarum Historia* George Buchanan rails against Mary, claiming that she indulged in *'sports that were clearly unsuitable to women'*.[3] Mary's half-brother, James Stewart, the Earl of Moray, who admittedly had no reason to love the Queen, was more specific in the *'Articles'* he put before the Westminster Commissioners on 6 December 1568.

> *Few dayes eftir the murther remaning at halyrudehous, she past to seytoun, exercing hir one day richt oppinlie at the feildis with the palmall and goif, And on the nicht planelie abusing hir body with boithuell.*[4]

According to Lord Moray, Mary played golf and 'palmall' at Seton shortly after Darnley's death, and dallied there with the Earl of Bothwell, the prime suspect in the explosion at Kirk o' Fields. 'Palmall' would seem to be the French game of 'jeu-de-mail' or 'paille-maille'. In one form it resembled croquet but there was also a long-driving cross-country form of the game similar to golf.

Leaving aside Mary's morals and the question of Darnley's sudden death, these extracts reveal something of attitudes towards women's golf in the 16th century when it would seem to have been considered as frivolous, slightly risqué, and certainly not a ladylike sport.

[3]   Cited in W.A. Gatherer, *The Tyrannous Reign of Mary, Queen of Scots* (Edinburgh, 1958), p. 120.
[4]   'Staying at Holyroodhouse for a few days after the murder, she then went to Seton, taking exercise one day right openly in the fields with palmall and golf, and at night clearly dallying with Bothwell.' British Library, Add. MS. 33531.

Mary's son, James VI and I, also took an interest in golf. Traditionally, he is believed to have learnt on the North Inch of Perth, and may well have continued to play in England when the Scottish court moved to London on James's accession to Elizabeth I's throne in 1603. He has been associated with the foundation of the Royal Blackheath Golf Club in 1608. The Club's records, however, were destroyed by fire in the late 18th century, and there is no documentary evidence for its existence prior to 1787.[5]

Although golf is not mentioned in the *Basilkon Doron*, James's instructions to his son, Prince Henry, in which he recommends games to '*exercise the engine*', the young prince was probably a golfer. It is recorded that on one occasion he came close to accidentally striking his schoolmaster with a raised club.[6] It has been claimed that a painting by an unknown Flemish artist depicting a child with a golf club and ball is Prince Henry, thus lending weight to the argument for the Dutch origin of the game.[7] However, both the age of the child, and the Breda medal he is wearing, make this improbable. Undoubtedly, there were close ties between the royal houses of Scotland and the Netherlands, and a representative of the States General stood godfather at the young Prince's christening at Stirling in 1549. Nonetheless, Dutch merchants traded in many countries. That golf did not flourish in East Anglia, for example, where they were frequent visitors, indicates that cultural and trading contacts with the Low Countries were not necessarily the reason for the development of golf in Scotland.

There is evidence that James VI and I took an interest in the developing trade in golfing equipment. William Mayne, '*bower burgess*' of Edinburgh, was appointed royal club-maker for life, and in 1618 James gave the patent of golf ball-making in Scotland to James Melville for twenty-one years in favour of the ball-maker, William Berwick, to '*furnische the said kingdom with better golf balls*'.

In the Letters of Licence of 1618, James shows his awareness of the importance of the game to the Scottish economy when he states that '*no small quantity of gold and silver is transported yearly out of Heines' [His Highness's] kingdom of Scotland for buying of golf balls*'. No indication of the source of these balls is given, but it seems likely to have been the Low Countries, as Dutch toll-registers for Bergen op Zoom for 1486 record that 'Ritsaert' [Richard] Clays paid six groats for exporting a barrel of golf balls to Scotland. Further examples of balls bought for sale in Scotland are recorded for 1494, 1495, and 1496.[8]

Ball-making was organised as a trade in the Low Countries from the mid-16th century when there is known to have been a system of apprenticeship in

James VI and I, from the frontispiece to his own work The Basilikon Doron, or His Maiesties instructions to his dearest sonne *(Edinburgh, 1599).*
National Library of Scotland.

Menu card of the Royal Blackheath Golf Club, 1938. Traditionally, golf has been played at Blackheath, near Greenwich, from 1603 when James VI and I and his Scottish court moved to London.
National Library of Scotland, Dep.375/36, by permission of the Royal Burgess Golfing Society, Edinburgh.

5   Ian T. Henderson and David I. Stirk, *Royal Blackheath* (London, 1981).
6   British Library, Harleian MS. 6391.
7   Ian T. Henderson and David I. Stirk, *Golf in the Making* (London, 1979), p. 8.
8   van Hengel, p. 51.

Letters of Licence to James Melville, 1618.
In 1618, James VI and I gave the patent of golf ball-making in Scotland to James Melville, Quarter-Master to the Earl of Morton.
Scottish Record Office, PS1/87, fols 169-70.

existence. In Goirle, a town whose inhabitants are still known by their nickname of *'ball-stuffers'*, a ball-maker is mentioned in a document of 1552. So prolific were the town's ball-makers that they were able to give immediate assistance to the nearby village of Tilburg when Sebastian van Warendrop, the army commander of the Duke of Parma in the Spanish War, demanded a ransom of 12,000 golf balls in 1588.[9]

It is not stated what type of balls were being made in Goirle at this time. If the Dutch game was played primarily on ice, it would require a very different ball from the featherie, as it would need to float, or at least not become mis-shapen through constant contact with ice. Wooden golf balls, such as the boxwood balls dating from the mid-16th century found under a house in Amsterdam, would have been suitable.

James Melville, given the patent of golf ball-making in Scotland by James VI and I in 1618, is unlikely to have been a ball-maker himself as he was Quarter-master to the Earl of Morton. He had partners and assistants who could lease his rights to craftsmen, but, in accordance with the terms of the monopoly, every ball produced had to bear Melville's stamp, and he was authorised to seek out and confiscate illegal ones. An entry in the Register of the Privy Council of Scotland for 1629, however, reveals that the patent was never enforced.

In that year, William Dickson and Thomas Dickson, golf ball-makers in Leith, complained to the Privy Council against James Melville for *'pretending*

---

[9] van Hengel, pp. 29-30.

he has a gift from his Majesty's late father, for exacting a "certain impost aff everie gowffe ball made within this kingdome" which gift their Lordships had never ratified, and on 20th February last, he sent a number of "lawlesse souldiers...who after manie threatnings and execrable oathes...tooke frome thame ane greate nomber of gowffe ballis quhilkis [which] they had made for his Majesteis use at the desire of Arthure Naismith, indweller in Edinburgh"'. The outcome was that *'the Lords find that James Melville and his servants took nineteen gowffe ballis from the pursuers most unwarrantably'.* Melville was fined and cautioned.[10]

The reign of Charles I, the last Stuart monarch born in Scotland, was a turbulent one which saw the religious upheavals of the Covenanting Movement in Scotland, the English Civil War, the King's flight to the Continent, his return and his subsequent capture. It ended dramatically with the King's execution in 1649. Nonethleless, in the midst of all this upheaval there were more peaceful moments, and when Charles received the news of the 1641 Irish Rebellion, legend has it he was playing golf on Leith Links.

It was on the same Links at Leith that what has been dubbed the first golf 'international' is said to have been played in 1681. The then Duke of York, later

Copy of Sir John Gilbert's 'Charles I on Leith Links, 1641', of 1876, on a 19th-century trophy of the Thistle Golf Club, Edinburgh. Legend has it that Charles I was playing golf on Leith Links when he received the news of the Irish Rebellion of 1641.
National Museums of Scotland.

[10]   *Register of the Privy Council of Scotland, 1629-30,* Vol. III, 2nd Series (Edinburgh, 1901), p. 174.

James Drummond 'Golfer's Land, Canongate, Edinburgh', c.1850.
The house in the Canongate of Edinburgh which James Drummond is supposed to have purchased following victory in the first golfing 'international' between Scotland and England.
Central Library, Edinburgh.

The escutcheon on Golfer's Land, Canongate, Edinburgh, from the Rules of the Thistle Golf Club *(Edinburgh, 1824).*
National Library of Scotland.

James VII, spent some time in Scotland between 1680 and 1682 as the King's Commissioner, residing at Holyroodhouse with his Duchess and for part of the time his daughter, the future Queen Anne. Tradition relates that he challenged two English noblemen to a game of golf following their claim that it was an English sport.

The Duke chose as his partner James Paterson, a cordiner or cobbler, and local golf champion. The Scots won the day, and the prize money enabled Paterson to acquire the house in the Canongate of Edinburgh which later became known as Golfer's Land. Legend has it that the Duke caused an escutcheon to be fixed on the house depicting a crest with the ducal hand holding a golf club and bearing the motto '*Far and Sure*'. Golfer's Land no longer stands, but a commemorative plaque has been placed on a nearby property.

As a postscript to this story, the Edinburgh Town Council minutes for 1723 show that George Fenwick, a brewer in Leith, had the right to a house on the South Leith Links feued by the town to the deceased James Paterson, Cordiner on the Canongate, for 5 merks or a set of golf clubs yearly to the Provost. The Council chose the clubs.[11]

Golf may have been banned by Act of Parliament, by Burgh Councils and by Kirk Sessions, but given that many of the Stuart kings themselves played this so-called '*unproffitable sport*', to attempt to ban the game can only have been a forlorn hope. Indeed, golf would seem to have been a deeply rooted national pastime for king and commoner alike from the 16th century onwards.

11 C.E.S. Chambers, 'Early Golf at Bruntsfield and Leith', in *Book of the Old Edinburgh Club*, Vol. XVIII (Edinburgh, 1932), p. 10.

Plan of St Andrews, attributed to John Geddy, c.1580.
Although this plan of St Andrews emphasizes the important educational and
ecclesiastical buildings at the eastern end of the town, the Links to the west, where
James Melville probably played his golf, are clearly shown.
National Library of Scotland, MS. 20996.

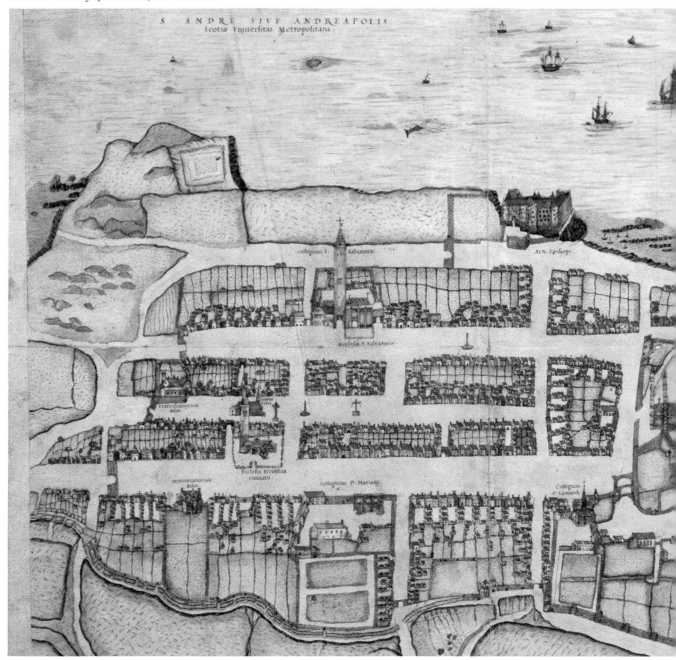

3 JAMES MELVILLE
THE ST ANDREWS STUDENT, 1574

AN EARLY GOLFING HISTORIAN, SIR WALTER SIMPSON, WRITING IN THE MID-19TH century, surmised that golf in St Andrews started when a shepherd idly hit a stone into a hole with his crook.[1] There is no firm evidence to substantiate this speculation, and written records of St Andrews golf date from 1552. Then, in an Acknowledgement of permissions granted to him by the Town Council, John Hamilton, Bishop of St Andrews, reserved to the people of the Burgh the right to use the Links for '*golfe, futeball, shuting and all games*', indicating that golf was already popular in the town.[2] According to Dutch documentary sources, there was trade in golfing equipment between Scotland and the Low Countries in the late 16th century: merchants from the Netherlands, Norway, and France are known to have visited the annual Senzie Fair in St Andrews held between 1350 and 1581, where it is tempting to suppose golf may have been one of their leisure activities.[3]

One of the most interesting documents to have survived from the early days of golf in St Andrews is a diary kept by a student at the University there.[4] James Melville was the son of the Minister of Maryton, near Montrose, on the north-east coast of Scotland. The nephew of the better known Andrew Melville, the famous preacher and theologian, he was a student between 1569 and 1574. Later he became Minister of Kilrenny in Fife, and was elected Moderator of the General Assembly of the Church of Scotland in 1589. He died in Berwick-upon-Tweed in 1614 while imprisoned by Charles I for his staunch opposition to that monarch's reintroduction of bishops into Scotland.

For much of his eventful life James Melville kept a 'Diary'. In this closely-written volume, which could more accurately be described as his 'memoirs', Melville gives important information about ecclesiastical and political happenings in Scotland from the presbyterian point of view at a turbulent time in the country's history, and it is for this that the diary is largely known. However, he also noted details of his personal and family life, providing us with a rare

[1] Sir Walter Simpson, *The Art of Golf* (Edinburgh, 1887).
[2] H.S.C. Everard, *A History of the Royal and Ancient Golf Club of St Andrews* (Edinburgh, 1907), pp. 28-30.
[3] van Hengel, p.12.
[4] National Library of Scotland, Adv. MS. 34.4.15. For a more detailed discussion of James Melville's diary see *The Diary of Mr James Melville*, Bannatyne Club (Edinburgh, 1829).

insight into daily life outside the classroom for a student at St Andrews in the late 16th century.

By his own account, James Melville appears to have been a hard-working and eager student, although, endearingly, he does record that when he first arrived classes might end in tears. He tells us he was neither well-grounded in Latin grammar nor particularly mature, and so failed to understand the Latin lessons. '*I did nathing bot bursted and grat...and was of mynd to haiff gone ham agean.*' Melville appears soon to have overcome his early problems and seems to have enjoyed his years as a student. He even found time for games, one such being golf.

In his diary, in addition to noting details of the academic courses he attended, his tutors, and visits to St Andrews from notables such as John Knox, Melville recorded his recreations. At school in Montrose the young Melville had been '*teached to handle the bow for archerie, the glub [club] for goff, the batons for fencing, also to rin [run], to loope [jump], to swoom [swim], to warsle [wrestle]*'. While he does not seem to have had a great deal of pocket money, Melville tells us his father provided him with the means to purchase his '*necessars*'. Thus, the young James had bow and arrows for archery, and club and balls for golf. Fatherly approval, however, did not extend to '*Catchpull and Tavern*', that is, hand tennis and drinking in taverns, but '*now and then*' he was able to play a game of '*racket catche*', another form of tennis.

No details are given in the diary of golfing equipment available in the St Andrews of 1574, save that James Melville had '*club and balls*', indicating that the game was perhaps played using a single club. Generally, little is known of the construction of early golf clubs: they may well have been made from one piece of wood cut out of a hedgerow. It is clear from later accounts, however, that the heads and shafts of clubs were made from different woods as heads were indeed replaced.

A golf club needed to have two main properties: a head of hardwood capable of withstanding many strikes of the ball, and also a whippy or springy shaft. These properties did not occur together in any natural British timber. A one-piece club would need to have a springy shaft. Springy timber by its very nature is easy to split or cleave, thus, a one-piece ash club would have a springy shaft but a head that would easily split after a few strokes. The earliest clubs that survive have hawthorn heads, and most commonly, ash or alder shafts, although Thomas Kincaid, writing in Edinburgh in 1687, recommended hazel.[5] Lancewood or lemonwood has also been recorded, certainly from the 17th century.[6]

---

[5] Diary of Thomas Kincaid, National Library of Scotland, Adv. MS. 32.7.7. See below pp. 37-41.
[6] I am indebted to Robert Gowland of Phillips Auction House, Chester, for information concerning early golf clubs.

Als I haid my necessars honestlie aneuche of my father bot nocht els; for archerie and goff I haid bow arrose glub and bals, but nocht a purss for Catchpull and Tauern, sic was his fatherlie wesdom for my weill. Yit now and then I lernit and usit sa mikle bathe of the hand and racket catcheas might serue for moderat and halsome exerceise of the body.

Also, I had my necessaries honestly enough from my father but nothing else; for archery and golf I had bow arrows club and balls, but not money for hand tennis or drinking, such was his fatherly wisdom for my well-being. Yet now and then I learned and used so much of racket tennis as might serve for moderate and wholesome exercise of the body.

For practical reasons, more than one ball was required, and it seems likely they were made from a hardwood such as turned boxwood. In an account of the seige of Kirkwall Castle in Orkney in 1614 the Earl of Caithness tells of '*cannone billetts [bullets] ....brokkin lyke goulfe balls upoune the castelle*'. Cannon balls would split into separate pieces like wooden balls, whereas leather balls would only split at the seams. The evidence from the Continent at this time, from both pictures and documents, is that there, too, wooden balls were used.[7]

James Melville does not tell us where he played his golf. However, Bishop Hamilton's Acknowledgement of 1552 indicates that the Links were a popular golfing ground in St Andrews as elsewhere, and it would seem likely that Melville played his golf there. Yet, in spite of the evidence for the emergence of designated areas for the game from the 16th century, there are records which indicate that, inevitably, golf continued to be played within towns and villages for some time to come.

As late as 1632 the Books of Adjournal, the record of the Justiciary Court, tell of the death of a Kelso man, Thomas Chatto, '*within the kirk zaird of Kelso upoun the first day of Februar last be geving him ane deidlie straik with ane golf ball struckin out with ane golf club under his left lug*'. This incident happened during a '*bonspill at the golf within the said kirk zaird*' when the unfortunate Chatto was '*lurking*' in the church yard at the time of the match. It seems likely that he was merely an innocent bystander.[8]

The evidence as to where golfers played in Scotland prior to the 18th century is condradictory, and it seems they sometimes went to open spaces and at other times played in confined areas. Possibly, the game was played in the streets by small children or by people who did not have the time to go out to a field or the links for a proper game. It is hardly surprising that, removed from the thoroughfares, golf was regarded more favourably as a pleasant recreation.

[7] Douglas Young, *St Andrews: Town and Gown, Royal and Ancient* (London, 1969), p. 122.
[8] *Selected Justiciary Cases, 1624-50*, Vol. I, Stair Society (Edinburgh, 1953), p. 204.

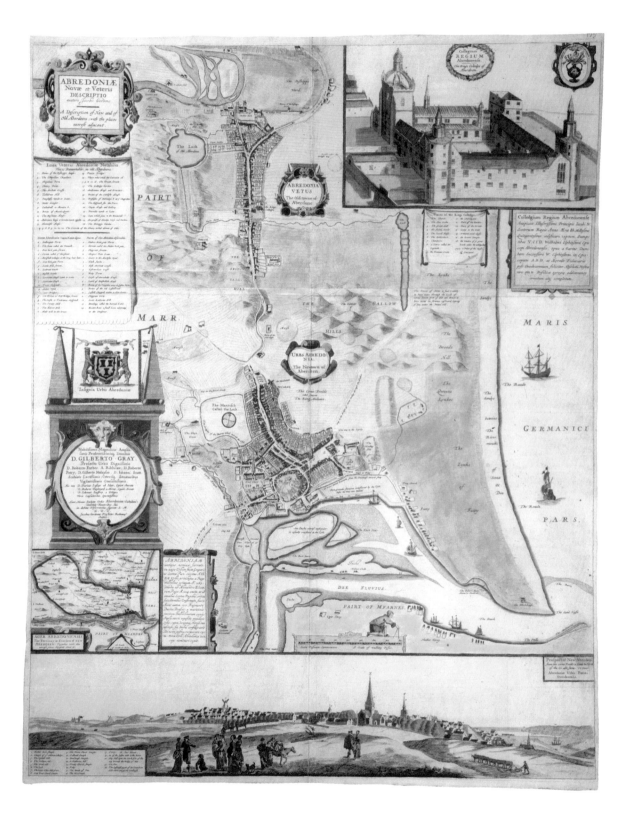

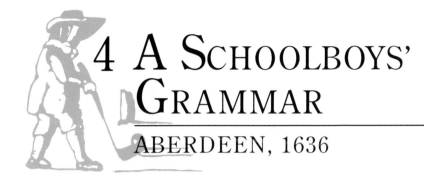

4 A Schoolboys' Grammar

Aberdeen, 1636

MUCH OF THE EARLY EVIDENCE FOR GOLF IN SCOTLAND SO FAR HAS CONCEN-
trated on the development of the game in the south and east of the country.
There is evidence, however, from records of Town Councils and of Kirk
Sessions, and the papers of Incorporations and of private individuals, to
indicate that golf was also played in the north from at least the 16th century.

The Aberdeen Burgh Records mention golfers in the streets as early as
1538, and in 1613 note the conviction of John Allan, bookbinder, *'for setting ane*
goiff ball in the kirk yeard, and striking the same against the kirk'. Possibly this
was merely an act of malice, but perhaps the church door was being used as
a target. In 1625, soldiers are recorded as exercising *'in the principall pairt of*
the linkes betwixct the first hole and the Queen's hole'.[1] This would indicate that
the game had developed considerably by this time, with a multiplicity of fixed,
named holes.

[1] *Extracts from the Accounts of the Burgh of Aberdeen*, Old Spalding Club (Aberdeen, 1852, et seq.).

Sir Robert Gordon of Gordonstoun by an unknown artist.
Scottish National Portrait Gallery.

Further north, Sir Robert Gordon of Gordonstoun, known as the '*wizard*' because of his preoccupation with scientific enquiry, enthused over the links at Dornoch in his 'Genealogy of the Earls of Sutherland' of 1628, describing them as '*the fairest and lairgest links (or grein feilds) of any part in Scotland*'. In Sir Robert's opinion, '*They do far surpasse the feilds off Montrois or Saint andrews*'. Perhaps this assertion of Dornoch's superiority should not be taken at its face value as he goes on to state '*Ther is not a rat in Sutherland, and if they do come thither in shippes from other parts (which often happeneth) they dye presenttlie how soone they do smell of the aire of that countrey: and (which is strange) there is great store anfd aboundance of them in Catheynes, the very next adiacent province*'.[2]

Along the sea-coast are 'the fairest and lairgest links (or grein feilds) of any part in Scotland, fit for archerie, goffing, ryding, and all other exercise; They do far surpasse the feilds off Montrois or Saint andrews.'

Sir Robert Gordon of Gordonstoun, 'Genealogy and Pedigree of the Earls of Sutherland', 1628.
In his not entirely impartial account of Sutherland, Sir Robert Gordon describes Dornoch Links as '*the fairest and lairgest links (or grein feilds) of any part in Scotland*'. *National Library of Scotland, Dep.314/2 by permission of the Countess of Sutherland.*

[2]   National Library of Scotland, Dep.314/2.

It is not known if Sir Robert was himself a golfer, but he was probably a competent archer as he won the prize of a Silver Arrow in a competition at the Palace of Holyroodhouse in 1617 organised during James VI and I's first visit to Scotland following his accession to the English throne. On the death of John, Earl of Sutherland, in 1615, Sir Robert had became Tutor or Guardian to his young nephew, John, now himself Earl of Sutherland. Sir Robert's accounts as Tutor, now in the National Library of Scotland, include payments for golfing equipment for the young Earl while at school in Dornoch. In 1619, £10 was spent '*this yeir for bowes, arrowes, golff clubbes, and balls with other necessars for his L[ordship's] exercise*'.[3]

Item ten poundis guven this yeir for bowes, arrowes, golff clubbes, and balls, with other necessars for his L[ordship's] exercise.

'Sir Robert Gordon His Tutor Coumpt Book', 1616-22.
In his account book as Tutor to the young Earl of Sutherland, Sir Robert Gordon notes payments for golfing equipment bought for the Earl while at school in Dornoch.
National Library of Scotland, Dep.313/1597 by permission of the Countess of Sutherland.

Golf is also known to have been played in Orkney in the 17th century. In 1685, James Dickson, writing from Kirkwall, requested a friend to '*remember to bring with you one dozen of common golf ballis to me and David Moncrieff*'. Similarly, there are references to golf in the journal of a 17th-century Orkney skipper, Patrick Traill of Elness.[4]

It is from Aberdeen, however, in what at first seems to be a rather unlikely source, that one of the most interesting and detailed documents relating to the development of golf in 17th-century Scotland appears, namely David Wedderburn's schoolboys' Grammar.

3   National Library of Scotland, Dep.313/1597.
4   B.H. Hossack, *Kirkwall in the Orkneys* (Kirkwall, 1900), pp. 125, 129.

In about 1636, David Wedderburn, Master of Aberdeen Grammar School, prepared a Latin Grammar for his pupils.[5] Shown here is a copy of the 1713 edition. As conversation at the school was conducted in Latin, there was a need for the pupils to be taught the Latin for words they might use every day. In the *Vocabula*, Wedderburn seems to have attempted to motivate his pupils by including Latin words and phrases for a variety of sports, one such being golf. Football, archery, and bowls are given similar treatment, indicating the range of sporting activities available to Aberdeen schoolboys in the mid-17th century. The short section on golf, headed '*Baculus*', meaning 'club', provides a detailed, and often humorous, description of the game. Its importance lies in that here, for the first time, we are given some indication of how golf was played at the time.

BACULUS

Baculus, pila clavaria, a Golf Ball; Fovea, a Goat [bunker]; Percute pilam baculo: Nimis curtasti hunc missum, This is too short a stroak; Pila tua devia est: Procul excussisti pilam, This is a good stroak Statumina pilam arena, Teaz [tee up] your Ball on the sand; Statumen, The Teaze; Frustra es, That is a miss, vel irritus hic conatus est. Percute pilam, sensim, Give the Ball but a little chap. Apposite, That is very well. Im-missa est pila in Foveam, the Ball is goated. Quomodo eum hinc elidam. Cedo baculum ferreum. Let see the Bunkard Club. Iam iterum frustra es, that is the second miss. Tertio, quarto, etc. Bene tibi cessit hic ictus, That is well stricken. Male tibi cessit hic ictus. Huc recta pilam dirige: Dirige recta versus foramen, Strike directly upon the hole. Percute pilam sursum versus, Strike up the hill: Percute deorsum versus, Strike down the hill: Ah praeterlapsa est foramen; Factum quod volui, I would not wish a better stroak; Immissa est in paludem, It is in the Myre: Recta evolavir, It hath flown directly on. Baculi caput, the head of the Club. Baculi caulis, The Club shaft. Baculi manubrium, The handle where the wippen [grip] is, Baculi filum, The wippen.

John Allan's conviction for striking a golf ball against the kirk door in Aberdeen in 1613 shows that the game was still played in the town in the early 17th century. As in Edinburgh and St Andrews, the evidence as to where golf was played is contradictory, and the *Vocabula*, with its description of the playing surface, and references to up the hill and down the hill, as well as the words for holes and bunkers, and sand for teeing off, indicates that, in 1636, Aberdeen schoolboys were playing their golf on the coastal links. This is confirmed by James Gordon of Rothiemay's '*Aberdoniae Utriusque Descriptio Topographica*' of 1661. He writes of the Links, '*Here the inhabitants recreate themselves with several kinds of exercises, such as football, golf, bowling and archery. Here likewise they walk for their health*'.[6]

David Wedderburn, Vocabula *(Aberdeen, 1636).*
Frontispiece and extract from David Wedderburn's Latin Grammar of 1636. The passage headed 'Baculus', meaning 'club', provides a detailed and often humorous description of the game of golf.
National Library of Scotland.

5   David Wedderburn, *Vocabula* (Aberdeen, 1636). For a more detailed discussion, see David Hamilton, *Early Aberdeen Golf* (Glasgow and Oxford, 1985).

6   James Gordon's manuscript is in the National Library of Scotland, Adv. MS. 34.2.8., fol. 98. For a translation see Cosmo Innes, *A Description of both Towns of Aberdeen*, in the Old Spalding Club (Edinburgh, 1842).

(Upper club)
A square toe iron with a curved face, probably late 17th-century. Earl of Wemyss.

(Lower club)
A heavy or deep faced spur toe iron, mid-17th-century. Earl of Wemyss.

Golf on the links would at first have been a cross-country sport, with players starting at one man-made or natural feature and attempting to reach another in the fewest number of strokes. Only when the game developed to the point where individual holes were generally recognised by players did golf courses as such emerge. Much of the information in the *Vocabula* regarding the playing surface appears in print probably for the first time, and indicates how the development of the game was influenced by the use of Scotland's eastern coastal strips or links. Bunkers and sand for teeing off, or teazing, are appropriate to links courses. The former occur naturally through the action of wind on the sandy surface, but their potential as a hazard in the game was quickly realised, and they were later incorporated in man-made courses.

There has been some controversy regarding the use of tees, as the earliest 'Rules of Golf' laid down by the Company of Gentlemen Golfers in 1744 state that '*your tee must be on the ground*'. Thomas Kincaid, writing in Edinburgh in 1687-8, however, appears to have used the method known to Wedderburn as he recommended that when learning to drive '*tie [tee] your ball at first pretty high from the ground*'.[7]

Items of golfing equipment are also referred to by Wedderburn, revealing that golf in Aberdeen was no longer a one club game, as different clubs for different shots are mentioned. The Dutch poet, Bredero, also tells of a choice of clubs available to the early 17th-century 'kolver' or golfer. These were, either a club of ash weighted with lead, or 'syne schotse kilk' (i.e. his Scottish club), probably made of boxwood with lead in the heel to give weight.

In Wedderburn's Aberdeen a '*baculus fereus*' or iron-headed club was in use. This is described here as the '*bunkard club*', presumably the club used to get out of a bunker. Iron-headed clubs of the time were crude and heavy, and were liable to burst expensive featherie balls. It seems likely they were used as a last resort to hit out of bunkers or very rough ground. Also of interest are the words given for different parts of the club: '*baculi caput*' is the head of the club, and '*baculi caulis*' the shaft, indicating the arrival of jointed clubs. It would seem the head and shaft were bound together with some form of fabric, the '*wippen*'. Wedderburn also says the '*wippen*' was on the handle, and the word seems to refer either to the fabric over the joint between head and shaft, or to the grip.

A golf ball is described here as a '*pila clavaria*', that is a ball like a skull. This is a featherie ball, the stitching of which resembled the bones on the top of the head. The featherie consisted of segments of leather, usually three, sewn together to form a bag and then stuffed with feathers, traditionally sufficient to fill the crown of a top hat. The pressure created added considerably to the ball's liveliness, and a well made featherie represented a significant techno-

---

[7]   For Thomas Kincaid's diary see below, pp. 37-41.

25

logical advance on the earlier wooden balls. The featherie was not without its faults: it quickly became sodden and heavy in wet conditions, easily lost its shape, and was liable to burst when miss-hit on a seam with an iron club. Featheries were also very expensive, as a ball-maker could only make three or four in a day. Despite this, the featherie is of great importance, and was favoured until the mid-19th century when it was replaced by the gutta ball.

The evidence as to the construction of golf balls in the late 16th and early 17th centuries is contradictory. The papers of the Canongate Cordiners (i.e.Cobblers) of Edinburgh refer to a dispute with the *'gouff ball makers'* of Leith in 1554 when the inference was that the cordiners were illegally stitching leather balls, but no further details of the construction of these balls is given. Featherie balls as such are known to have been in use by 1618 when James VI and I granted the twenty-one year monopoly of the golf ball trade in Scotland to James Melville (for which see Chapter 2), and it would seem safe to say a variety of balls were in use including wooden and stitched leather balls.

In 1642, by which time Melville's monopoly had expired, Aberdeen had its own golf ball-maker, John Dickson of Leith. He was a member of the rival firm of golf ball-makers who had complained to the Privy Council of Melville's high-handed actions in 1629. This unpleasantness behind him, Aberdeen Burgh Coucil gave Dickson a *'licence...of making gouff balls during the concils pleasure and his gude carage and behaviour, bacause there is no such tradesmen in this burgh and [he] has a testificat from Leith of his bygane life and conversation among them'*.[8] By the mid-17th century, golf balls were being made in several Scottish burghs including Leith, St Andrews, and Montrose as well as Aberdeen.

The *Vocabula* reveals that a variety of strokes were in use in 1636, including short strokes or putts and strokes up the hill and down the hill. Wedderburn also gives a number of common phrases for use when on the course. Most, such as *'Bene tibi cessit hic ictus'* — *Well struck!* — might still be heard today, although it is to be hoped that modern players do not need to use the phrase *'Immissa est in paludem - It is in the myre!'*.

---

[8]   Aberdeen Burgh Records.

5 'POOR MASTER GALL'

PERTH, 1638

IN 1638, HENRY ADAMSON'S *The Muses Threnodie, Or Mirthfull Mournings on the Death of Master Gall* was published in Edinburgh.[1] Adamson's verses are among the earliest printed works to mention golf. They also confirm that the game was popular in Perth in the lifetime of James Gall, the Master Gall of the title.

This is not the earliest known reference to golf in Perth, as according to the Lord High Treasurer for Scotland's Accounts, James IV paid fourteen shillings in 1502 for clubs from a *'bowar'* or bow-maker in St Johnston, or Perth.[2] As bow-makers were used to working in wood, it has been assumed that they had the skill and the equipment necessary to make wooden golf clubs, and that as demand for bows and arrows declined, so club-making took over. There is no written evidence to substantiate this, but it is known that later, when iron clubs became more common, they were made by blacksmiths.

The Lord High Treasurer's Accounts do not indicate where in Perth James IV played his golf. Situated on the banks of the Firth of Tay, Perth is not a coastal town and has no links. The town's Kirk Session minutes from 1592,

---

[1]   Henry Adamson, *The Muses Threnodie, or Mirthfull Mournings on the Death of Master Gall* (Edinburgh, 1638).
[2]   Scottish Record Office, E21.

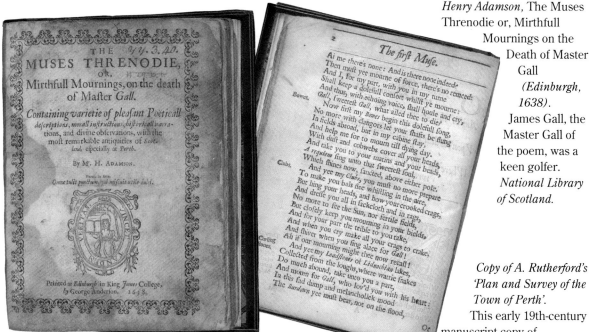

Henry Adamson, The Muses Threnodie or, Mirthfull Mournings on the Death of Master Gall (Edinburgh, 1638). James Gall, the Master Gall of the poem, was a keen golfer. National Library of Scotland.

Club And yee my Clubs, you must no more prepare
To make you bals flee whistling in the aire,
But hing [hang] your heads, and bow your crooked crags [necks],
And dresse you all in sackcloth and in rags,
No more to see the Sun, nor fertile fields,
But closely keep you mourning in your bields [shelters],
And for your part the trible [treble] to you take,
And when you cry make all your crags to crake [shake],
And shiver when you sing alace for Gall!
Ah if our mourning might thee now recall!

Copy of A. Rutherford's 'Plan and Survey of the Town of Perth'.
This early 19th-century manuscript copy of Rutherford's map of Perth was appended to the 1774 edition of the *Muses Threnodie* in the National Library of Scotland. The North Inch where Master Gall probably played his golf is on the right-hand side. National Library of Scotland.

however, make reference to golf on the Muirton meadows, near to the North Inch, and James IV may well have played there.

In his poem of 1638, Henry Adamson mourns the death of his friend, James Gall, whom he describes fulsomely as '*a citizen of Perth, and a gentleman of goodly stature, and pregnant wit, much given to pastimes such as golf, archerie, and curling; and Joviall companie*'. Master Gall was a committed sportsman who regularly played golf, shot, and curled. If the proportion of the poem devoted to the respective sports is any indication, archery was his first love, but golf and curling seem to have come a close second.

A footnote to the 1774 edition of Henry Adamson's lament for his friend elaborates on the subject of golf: '*Perth stands in the middle of a beautiful green about an English mile in length, where the citizens for ages have exercised themselves during the spring and autumnal seasons with golf clubs and balls. The pastime is interrupted during the summer months by the luxuriency of the grass...milch cows, etc*'.

Adriaen van de Velde, 'Golfers on the Ice near Haarlem',
1668
This landscape painting of 1668 depicts golfers on the ice near Haarlem. Two of the players are shown wearing kilts, and it may be they were Scottish merchants or soldiers who happened to be in the Low Countries.
National Gallery.

In the Low Countries too, golf was played largely from autumn until spring, partly because in the summer the long grass made it difficult to locate balls. In 1483, however, the Mayors of Haarlem granted the mowing rights of the golf course to the 'Masters of the Hours' of the parish church, providing the course remained in use as a playing field.[3] Haarlem it would seem was exceptional, and generally, at least in the days before areas were specifically set aside for the game, golf was a seasonal activity, with play being dictated as much by the other uses of the course as the leisure time of the players.

In 17th-century Scotland it was normal for golfing grounds to be used for many other purposes. Greens such as that in Perth were treated as common land where animals might graze. They might also be used as drying grounds for laundry. Recreation was but one use to which these areas might be put, and golf was only one sport among many. The coastal links too had many functions. As early as 1552 the St Andrews Links were set aside for *'golfe, futeball, shuting and all games'* (see above p. 17). Leith Links were a well-known venue for archers, and the Races there were a regular feature of the Scottish sporting and social calendar until they were transferred to Musselburgh in 1816. Musselburgh too, is an example of Links being used as a play ground for all. With so many activities taking place, it is to be wondered if such areas were actually any safer than the streets and kirk yards had been in the past.

Given the evidence for golf on Scotland's eastern coast from Edinburgh and Leith to Aberdeen and Dornoch, it is hardly surprising to find the game was played elsewhere in north-east Scotland in the 17th century. One keen golfer who is known to have played at a number of places along this coast was the 1st Marquis of Montrose.

---

[3]   van Hengel, p. 20.

29

Born James Graham, the 1st Marquis of Montrose is arguably one of the most controversial of 17th-century Scots. His long and eventful career as soldier, statesman, and politician ended in 1650 when he was hanged as a traitor in the Grassmarket, Edinburgh. As a young man, Montrose was a noted sportsman: his prowess as an archer is well known as he won the prize of the Silver Arrow at St Andrews. The family account books reveal that the Marquis was also a golfer playing at Arbroath, Montrose, and St Andrews in the late 1620s.[4]

In 1628, Montrose went to St Andrews University where his financial affairs were managed by a '*pursemaster*', Mr John Lambie. Lambie's detailed accounts provide a remarkable picture of Montrose's life at the University, and in particular, of his recreations. The Marquis's favourite sport was undoubtedly archery, and his room is said to have been hung with bows. He also played golf on the Links at St Andrews and Leith, regularly visited the Races at nearby Cupar, hawked, hunted, and played tennis at Leith.

So fond of golf was Montrose that he played the day before his marriage to '*sweet Mistress Magdalene Carnegie*', and his accounts record: '*Item, the nynthe day [9 November 1629] in Montrois, my Lord playing at the golf with the Laird of Lusse, for two golf balls...24sh*'. Only a few days after the wedding the Marquis sent to St Andrews for new golfing equipment and repairs to his old clubs: '*Item, the nynteen day to ane boy going to St Andrews for clubs and bals to my Lord...32sh. Item, for sax new clubs and dressing som auld clubs, and for balls...11 lib. 8sh*'.

The accounts mention a St Andrews club-maker, James Pett, by name '*for furnishing my Lord with bows and arrows and clubs that year 7 lib. 8 sh*'. Pett is described as a '*bower*' in the accounts, indicating that bow-makers were making golf clubs in St Andrews in the 1620s, as they had in 1502 when James IV played at Perth.

Further north, in Banffshire in 1690, James Ogilvie wrote from Boyne to his cousins in Cullen inviting them to play '*long gouf*' on the sea braes near Boyne Castle. This letter would suggest the cousins met regularly for golf. James Ogilvy left it to the others to choose where they were to play, although he hints the Links at Boyne were better than those near Cullen House, the home of the Earl of Seafield, where his cousins lived. It seems they, too, had more than one club available as reference is made to '*your short putting club*'. Ogilvy ends with a gentle jibe concerning a game played by the cousins earlier at Eden in Aberdeenshire, which presumably was a sore point with Mr Patrick and his brother: '*we shall see ife ye cannot make better use of a club in this countrey then ye did at Eden*'.

March 1629

Item, for balls in the tinnes [tennis] court of Leith...16sh.

Item, for two goffe balls, my Lord going to the goffe ther...10sh.

Ife Mr. Patrick and you have a mind for a touch at long gouff tomorrow Lett me know this night wher I shall waitt on you with a second, or if yee would do me the honour to come this lenth [length], because the links ar better, and we shall see ife ye cannot make better use of a club in this countrey then ye did at Eden. this is not that I doubt but ye made good use of your short putting club ther.[5]

[4]   Mark Napier, *Memorials of Montrose and his Times*, Maitland Club (Edinburgh, 1848), Vol I, pp. 156-201.
[5]   Scottish Record Office, GD 248.

Jan Anthonisz van Ravesteyn, 'Portrait of a young boy with a golf club and ball', 1626. Courtesy of Sotheby's.

6 An Edinburgh Sportsman

SIR JOHN FOULIS OF RAVELSTON, 1686

SIR JOHN FOULIS OF RAVELSTON WAS A KEEN SPORTSMAN WHO KEPT A meticulous record of his everyday expenditure in a series of nine pocket-sized account books. Numbers 2 and 3 in the series, covering the years 1684-9, came to the National Library of Scotland in 1936 with the Liston Foulis papers.[1] These account books are the two volumes said to be missing by A.W.C. Hallen in his 1894 edition of Sir John's accounts for the Scottish History Society.[2]

Account Books of Sir John Foulis of Ravelston, 1684-9.
Sir John Foulis of Ravelston's account books provide a detailed record of his daily expenditure, including his regular game of golf on Leith Links.
National Library of Scotland, MSS. 6153-4.

FACING PAGE
David Allan, 'William Inglis on Leith Links', 1787.
This painting shows William Inglis on Leith Links in 1787, some hundred years after Sir John Foulis played there. In the background is the Procession of the Silver Club, for which prize the members of the Company of Gentlemen Golfers competed.
Scottish National Portrait Gallery.

A country gentleman with an estate at Ravelston, then a few miles outside Edinburgh, Sir John was a keen sportsman. The accounts tell of Sir John's life in the country and in Edinburgh where he spent much time both on business and pleasure. Sir John held the office of Keeper of the Register of Sasines and had his town house in Foster's Wynd. There is much information about Sir John's large family by his four wives, his friends and acquaintancies, and his pastimes and recreations. The overall impression given is of a conscientious, caring family man, a sociable person with many friends who participated in a wide range of recreations; above all Sir John Foulis was a man who enjoyed life.

[1] National Library of Scotland, MSS. 6153-4.
[2] A.W.C. Hallen, *The Account Book of Sir John Foulis of Ravelston, 1671-1707*, Scottish History Society (Edinburgh, 1894).

Amusements feature large in the accounts. Sir John enjoyed many of the field sports popular with country gentlemen at the end of the 17th century. He hunted hares with hounds, kept greyhounds, probably for coursing, and hawked and fished on his estate at Ravelston. We also know that he was a regular bowler at Potterow in Edinburgh, and that while in town he diced and played cards. Gossip with friends in taverns and other meeting places seems to have been a regular indulgence. Sir John also enjoyed horse racing and rarely missed the annual spring race meeting at Leith. He seems to have been somewhat less fond of curling, though, as the sport is mentioned only occasionally. Given this range of sporting activities and the proximity of the Links at Leith to Ravelston, it is hardly surprising that Sir John was also a golfer.

Golf seems to have been Sir John's favourite sport, and he played regularly at Leith. His accounts do not give a great deal of information as to how the game was played, but they are of value in other ways. A golf ball bought in Leith in the 1680s cost 5 shillings, and clubs 10 shillings. There are references to different types of clubs, such as 'my play club' and a 'lead scraper club' on 30 January 1686. On that date, Sir John had a new head fixed to his lead club and the play club mended for a total of 14 shillings. It has been estimated that clubs lasted on average only ten rounds.[4] Then as now, golfing equipment was expensive, and even a gentleman of considerable means is seen taking the trouble to have his clubs repaired and renewed.

On 22 December, 1686, Sir John made a payment of 4 shillings 'for carieing my clubs'. Caddies are mentioned in connection with golf from the early 16th century. The Marquis of Montrose had employed a boy to carry his clubs in 1628, and Andrew Dickson was named as the future James VII and II's caddy when he played at Leith in 1681. Until at least the 18th century, however, a 'caddy' meant a porter or someone who ran errands, and did not specifically refer to a person who carried golf clubs. Bags were not regularly used until the last decade of the 19th century, and Sir John's caddy would have simply tucked the clubs under his arm much as a sporting gun might be carried.

Sir John seems to have enjoyed the social aspect of his sport. His account books regularly record the names of his companions, how much he wagered on the outcome of a game, and details of the entertainment enjoyed afterwards. The extract for 22 December 1686 shows that on this occasion Sir John's golfing companion was Sir George Mackenzie, later Earl of Cromartie. Mackenzie, described here by his office as Lord Clerk Register, paid for supper after the game. The coachman too is not forgotten, and the purchase of his measure of ale is recorded along with a new ball and Sir John's loan to

---

Extracts from Sir John Foulis of Ravelston's Account Books, 1686-9.
National Library of Scotland, MSS. 6153-4.

[30 Jan. 1686]
to malcolme to pay for a new head to a Lead Scraper club[3] & mending my play club   00:14:0
Lent to mrs dunbar   29:0:0
Spent at golf and coatch hyres [coach hires] and Supper wt [with] moncreife [and] Inglistone etc.   3:15:0

[22 Dec. 1686]
for a golfe ball the coachmans chopine eall [measure of ale], & lent to L[ord] Clerk]: Register for a horne to his club & [to the] poor folk   0:8:0
for carieing [carrying] my clubs   0:4:0
my Lord register payed our Supper

---

3   Probably a spooned club with a leaded heel.
4   David Hamilton, *Early Golf at St Andrews* (Glasgow, 1986), p. 26.

'Copy of the Life of Sir Robert Sibbald, MD..., 1805'.
While returning from a visit to a patient in Leith in 1690, Sir Robert Sibbald was set upon by a boy wielding a golf club.
National Library of Scotland, Adv. MS. 33.5.1., p 72.

Mackenzie to purchase a '*horne to his club*'. Other companions of Sir John's over the years were drawn from the leading political and legal figures of the time, and include Sir John Baird of Newbyth, Sir Archibald Primrose, and Sir Peter Wedderburn of Gosford. Often, four or five names might be given followed by an '*etc*', suggesting Foulis was listing a few notables among the company and that a considerable number of golfers had gone out to play that day.

Sir John played his golf entirely during the winter and usually at weekends. In the four months from December 1685 to the end of March 1686, he records eight outings to play on Leith Links, indicating a game about once a fortnight. He may well have played more often, as on several other occasions Sir John spent time with his golfing cronies but does not specify for what activity, if any, they met. The bill for the eight golfing outings came to £21 10 shillings for equipment, wagers, coach hire, and entertainment in the form of food and drink. Unfortunately, the accounts often record only total expenditure, and so it is not possible to calculate how much he spent on golfing equipment alone.

Sir John Foulis's account books give the impression of golf as a thoroughly enjoyable recreation far removed from the image of the game as a rowdy and dangerous pastime as earlier records suggest. There were, however, still risks attached to the sport in the late 17th- century as there are today. Writing in his autobiography in 1690, Sir Robert Sibbald, the physician and antiquary, noted in graphic medical detail an unprovoked attack made on him while he was returning home from visiting a patient in Leith.[5]

Ane accident befell me the 16 of October 1690 that as I was coming from Sir Robert Milne his house in Leith, where I had been visiting his Good Brother Mr. Elphiston's wyfe, who had taken physick that day, about four afternoon as I was going down to passe the Ditch to goe to the Links wher I left some Company playing at Goufe & my servant following me, neither he nor I nor the boy adverting I was strucken wt the back of the Club wt much force betwixt the Eyes at the root of the nose, the wound was oblong large, and about half ane inch long it was not half ane inch above the cartilage of the nose, the parts under the right eye was livid, and both the Canthi Majores were swelled I bled much & took a coach & came up, & was a good whyl befor I could want a plaister upon it. It was God his great goodness that neither the Cartilage was cut nor one of ye Eye putt out for it was done with the sharpe syde of the Club.

5   National Library of Scotland, Adv. MS. 33.5.1., pp. 72-3. The original manuscript of Sibbald's autobiography appears to be lost. This copy was made in 1805.

[26 Jan. 1687]

...I thought on the playing

1   *at the Golve. I found that, ye most rest most upon the right*
    legg for the most part but yet not too much for as to be exactly
    perpendicular upon it, which ye will know by the ballance

2   *ing of your body. 2 I found that the club most always move*
    in a circle makeing ane angle of 45 degrees with the

3   *horizon. 3 That the whole turning of your body about most*
    be by thrawing the joynts of your right legg and then when
    [missing]...you most thraw the
        thraw the small of your back so that the left shoulder
    will turn a little down wards, because the body is inclined a
    little forward, but ye most beware of raising the on shoulder
    higher than the other as to their position in the body, for
    that motion is not convenient for this action. 4 I found
    that in bringing down the club ye most turn your body
    as farr about towards the left following the swinge of the club
    as it had been turned before towards the right hand.

4   *Extract from Thomas*
    Kincaid's diary, 1687-8.
    National Library of Scotland,
    Adv. MS. 32.7.7.

7 THOMAS KINCAID

DIARY OF AN EDINBURGH MEDICAL STUDENT, 1687-8

AT ABOUT THE SAME TIME AS SIR JOHN FOULIS WAS ENJOYING HIS REGULAR, social, round of golf with his cronies on Leith Links, a young Edinburgh medical student, Thomas Kincaid, was taking the game far more seriously. In his diary, Kincaid analyses and describes the game, and in doing so produces the earliest known written set of golfing instructions.[1]

The son of a surgeon-apothecary, Thomas Kincaid studied medicine in Edinburgh in the mid-1680s. His diary covers only a few months from January 1687 to December 1688; however, this is no ordinary journal of social engagements. Rather, Thomas seems to have meditated, usually in the small hours, on a wide range of subjects, later confiding his 'thoughts' to his diary. So, day after day, the diary begins, 'Today I thought upon...' and Thomas proceeds to write up his myriad reflections in considerable detail. As might be expected, there is much relating to medicine, but the young Thomas seems to have had an enquiring mind with many interests including theology, literature, politics, music, and sport, to name but a few.

Golf and archery were Thomas Kincaid's main sporting activities, and he makes frequent reference to both. Kincaid's career as an archer is better recorded than his prowess as a golfer, and it is known that in later life he was a member of the Royal Company of Archers and won the Edinburgh Silver Arrow in 1711. The golf instructions in the diary occur in the January and February of 1687, when Kincaid notes regular forays on the links. Like Sir John Foulis, Thomas Kincaid played golf during the winter months. They also shared a preference for Leith Links, but Bruntsfield Links, much nearer to his Edinburgh lodgings than Leith, are mentioned too, and it seems likely he also played there.

Much of what is known of Bruntsfield Links at the time comes from the English artist, Paul Sandby. Sandby was employed in the military drawing department at the Tower of London from 1741, and in 1746 was in Scotland as a draughtsman on the Highland survey commissioned to strengthen the army in Scotland against further Jacobite activities. Sandby's survey drawings

1   Diary of Thomas Kincaid, 1687-8, National Library of Scotland, Adv. MS. 32.7.7. For a more detailed discussion of Thomas Kincaid's diary, see Henry W. Meikle, 'An Edinburgh Diary' in *Book of the Old Edinburgh Club*, Vol. 27 (Edinburgh, 1949), pp. 111-54.

FACING PAGE
*Paul Sandby, 'A View of Bruntsfield Links Looking Towards Edinburgh Castle',
1746.*
Bruntsfield Links, then about a mile outside Edinburgh, were a popular golfing ground, probably from the 16th century, but as Sandby's 'View' indicates, conditions were not ideal.
British Museum.

*12 [November 1687]
Satt[urday] I went out and walked with Hen: Legatt thro[ugh] Bruntsfield Links...*

presented to the Board of Ordnance are now in the British Museum. The view shown on p.36, made during his time in Scotland, depicts Edinburgh Castle perched above the town with Bruntsfield Links in the foreground. A group of figures, possibly soldiers with their caddies, are playing golf. As Sandby's pictures are known for their topographical accuracy, it seems probable he actually witnessed a game of golf taking place.

Bruntsfield Links were at the time about a mile outside Edinburgh. They were quarried from at least 1508, and as a result were soon indented with large holes from which the soft, grey sandstone which typifies many of the buildings in the city and Leith was extracted. The remaining areas were used by the citizens for golf, while the quarries, one of which is visible in Paul Sandby's picture, were utilised as bunkers. The Edinburgh Burgh records indicate the importance attached to the area as a golfing ground since many of the tacks, or leases, of parts of the Links reserve the rights of golfers.[2]

In 1723, the lease to John Paterson to graze his cattle on the Links reserved the right to play golf, to walk on the Links, to dry clothes in the bushes, to muster troops, and to use the springs of water. The records also reveal the poor condition of the Links for golf with descriptions of rocky areas, bogs, gorse, and whin. The area was not cleared until the mid-18th century.[3] Given the condition of Bruntsfield Links, it is perhaps understandable that, so often,

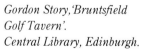

Gordon Story, 'Bruntsfield Golf Tavern'. Central Library, Edinburgh.

---

[2] *Extracts from the Records of the Burgh of Edinburgh 1701-18*, Scottish Burgh Record Society (London, 1967), pp. 62, 215.

[3] C.E.S. Chambers, 'Early Golf at Bruntsfield and Leith', in *Book of the Old Edinburgh Club* (Edinburgh, 1932), Vol. 18, pp. 1-10.

Kincaid and other residents of Edinburgh seem to have preferred to play at nearby Leith.

Despite the poor condition of the Links at Bruntsfield, there is little doubt that they were regularly used for golf, as Allan Ramsay's *Elegy on Maggy Johnston who died Anno 1711* testifies.[4] Maggy Johnston kept a tavern at the edge of Bruntsfield Links, which Ramsay tells us was so popular that '*Of Customers she had a Bang [a great number]; For Lairds and Souters [commoners] a[ll] did gang To drink bedeen, The Barn and Yard was aft sae thrang [crowded], We took the Green*'. Ramsay continues mournfully, '*Whan we were weary'd at the Gouff, Then Maggy Johnston's was our Houff [tavern]; Now a[ll] our Gamesters*

Allan Ramsay, Elegy on Maggy Johnston Who died Anno 1711 *(Edinburgh, 1718), p.1.*
Here, Allan Ramsay tells of large numbers of golfers on Bruntsfield Links.
National Library of Scotland.

> Right swash I trow,
> Then of auld Stories we did cant,
> Whan we were fou.
>
> Whan we were weary'd at the Gouff,
> Then *MAGGY JOHNSTON*'s was our Houff,
> Now a our Gamesters may sit douff,
> Wi Hearts like Lead.
> Death wi his Rung rax'd her a Youff,
> And sae she died.
>
> Maun

[*players*] *may sit douff [melancholy], Wi' Hearts like Lead, Death wi' his Rung rax'd her a Youff [Death with his stick reached her a blow], And sae she died*'.

Ramsay's lament for Maggy Johnston may make reference to golf on Bruntsfield Links, but it is to Thomas Kincaid's diary we must turn for a detailed set of instructions on how the game should be played. The extracts quoted from the diary form only a fraction of his thoughts on golf, yet they alone indicate how he analyses his game in minute detail down to the positioning of the body, the grip on the club, and the angle of swing. On 26 January 1687, he describes and analyses his very flat swing. This is appropriate to the clubs of the time, which were generally long and heavy by modern standards.

Kincaid was equally adamant about the construction of his golfing equipment. Concerning golf clubs he wrote: '*the shaft of your club most be made of hazell. Your club most be almost straight that is the head most make a verie obtuse angle with the shaft, and it most bend as much at the handle as it does at the wooping [the grip], being verie supple and both long and great*'. No hazel-shafted

---

4   Allan Ramsay, *Elegy on Maggy Johnston Who died Anno 1711* (Edinburgh, 1718), pp. 1-4.

clubs have as yet been discovered. All known 17th-century wooden clubs are ash, with the exception of a few lead clubs with alder shafts.

Kincaid records some purchases of golfing equipment. During early February 1687 he was ill, but by the 8th of the month, when he received a visit from his friend and golfing companion Henry Legatt, he felt well enough to rise from his sick bed and took the coach to Leith. There, Legatt 'bought a club in Captain Foster's', and later Kincaid bought three balls for 14 shillings.

> Hen: Legatt came in and desired me out to the golve. I putt on my cloths, and went to him he bought a club at Captain Foster's we went down to Leith In a Coach which was 10 shill[ings] we played till 5 I bought three balls 14 shil[ings] we went to Captain Brown's where we settled waiting on the coach but could not gett it...I was exceeding seek.

In spite of his stringent requirements for golfing equipment, Kincaid attempted his own repairs. On 25 January 1687 he notes: 'I glewed the club head... after dinner I took out the plains and made a little skelpe [splinter] to putt on the club. I took of the peice that was joynd to the old shaft. I glewed too that skelpe'.

A variety of golf balls seem to have been available. Kincaid recommends that 'your ball most be of a middle size nither to big nor too little, and then the heivier it is in respect of its bigness it is still the better. It most be of thick and hard leather not with pores or grains or that will let a pin easily passe throughe it especially at the soft end'. As well as attempting his own club repairs, Kincaid experimented with golf balls, colouring 'a golve ball with white lead'. Among the failings of the featherie ball was that it was porous and easily lost its shape and resilience in wet weather. Colouring the ball with white lead served the dual purpose of making the ball more conspicuous and less liable to take in water.

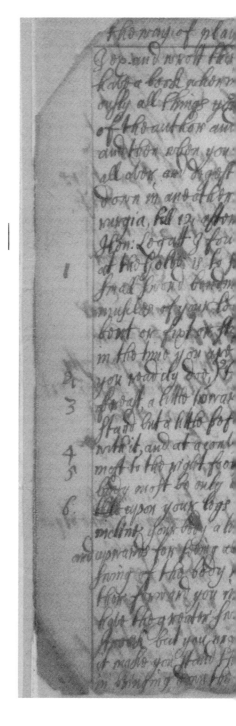

Diary of Thomas Kincaid, 1687-8.
Thomas Kincaid's diary includes the earliest known set of golfing instructions.
National Library of Scotland, Adv. MS. 32.7.7.

[20 Jan. 1687]
> ...after dinner I went out to the Golve with
> Hen: Legatt I found that the only way of playing
> 1   at the Golve is to stand as you do at fenceing with the
> small sword bending your legs a little and holding the
> muscles of your legs and back and armes exceeding
> bent or fixt or stiffe and not at all slackning them
> in the time you are bringing down the stroak (which
> 2   you readily doe,) the ball most be straight before your
> 3   breast, a little towards the left foot 3 your left foot most
> stand but a little before the right, or rather it most be even
> 4   with it, and at a convenient distance from it, 4 ye most lean
> 5   most to the right foot, 5 but all the turning about of your
> body most be only...
> upon your legs holding them as stiff as ye can...

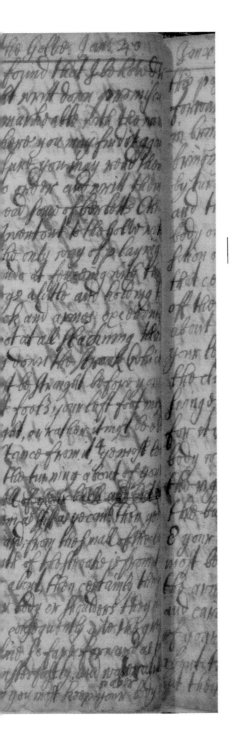

Also of interest are Kincaid's thoughts on what appears to be an early handicap system. '*Jan. 21... I thought upon the question whither it is better in giveing advantadge in gameing to make the game equal and the stakes unequal, or to make the stakes equal and give some advantadge in the game; as at the golve whither it is better to give a man two holes of three, laying equal stakes, or to lay three stakes to his on and equal for so much every hole.*' He concludes here that '*with these that are worst gamesters than yourselfe, make always the game depend upon moe hazards than on, and the moe the better; but with these that are better gamesters make always the game to depend only upon on hazard*'.

The final section on golf in the diary takes the form of a poem. Again, this seems to be a 'first' for Kincaid. Other 17th-century poems, including Henry Adamson's *The Muses Threnodie* of 1638, mention golf (Chapter 5), but this may well be the first poem entirely devoted to golf. On 9 February 1687, Thomas Kincaid's thoughts seem to have been darting from one subject to another in typical fashion before he gathered them together and wrote:

> *9 Wed. I rose at 7. I thought upon the method of pathologie, and on*
> *playing at the golve...I digested the rules of playing at the golve*
> *into verse thus.*
> *Gripe fast stand with your left leg first not farr*
> *Incline your back and shoulders but beware*
> *You raise them not when back the club you bring*
> *Make all the motion with your bodies swinge*
> *And shoulders, holding still the muscles bent*
> *Play slowly first till you the way have learnt*
> *At such lenth hold the club as fitts your strenth*
> *The lighter head requires the longer lenth*
> *That circle wherein moves your club and hands*
> *At forty five degrees from th horizon stands*
> *What at on stroak to effectuat you dispaire*
> *Seek only 'gainst the nixt it to prepare.*

Elsewhere in the diary, Kincaid describes his method as '*the only way of playing at the golve*'. Whether or not other golfers agreed with him is not known, as no comparable series of instructions for this time exists. What can be said, is that in writing down his '*thoughts*' on golf, Thomas Kincaid anticipated the first published golfing poem, Thomas Mathison's *The Goff*, of 1743, by over fifty years (Chapter 10), and the first printed book of golf instruction, H.B. Farnie's *The Golfer's Manual, By a Keen Hand*, published in 1857, by a hundred and seventy years.

Receive from the bearer our post
ane Sett of Golfe-Clubs consisting of three, viz. an play club,[1]
ane Scraper,[2] and ane tin fac'd club.[3] I might have made the set
to consist of more: but I know not your play and if you
stand in need of more I think you should call for
them from me. Tho I know you may be served
thear yet I presumed that such a present from this place
the metropolis of Golfing may not be unsuitable for these fields
especially when it's come from a friend. Upon the same
consideration I have also sent you ane Dozen of
Golfe balls which receive with the clubs. I am
told they are good, but that will prove according to your play
and the fields. If the size do not suite, were you so free with me
I would mend it with the next. I am glad to have any
occasion to kisse your hands at a distance And to
Subscribe my selfe still
St Andrews 27 April   Sir
*   1691   Your faithfull and most humble servant*
*   Al. Monro*

The bearer may have other Clubs and balls from
this place but yours cannot be mistaken
if you receive them marked viz.
The Clubs with the Letters G.M. as to the trades man's
proper signe for himselfe, and JMK for your mark stamped
upon ilke ane of the Clubs
And ilke ane of the balls are marked W.B. which
are not ordinarily counterfeited.

---

[1] A driving wood.   [2] A lofting wood.   [3] Probably an iron club.

8 ST ANDREWS

'THE METROPOLIS OF GOLFING', 1691–1716

THE MACKENZIE OF DELVINE PAPERS NOW IN THE NATIONAL LIBRARY OF Scotland have a curious history in that at some point, probably in the early 19th century, the door of the cupboard in which they had been placed was papered over. The papers were forgotten about and were only discovered accidentally by the butler at Delvine House, near Dunkeld in Perthshire, in 1918. These are the papers of a family of lawyers, at least one of whom was a golfer.[4]

John Mackenzie was the third son of Sir Kenneth Mackenzie, the 1st Baronet of Coul. Admitted to the Faculty of Advocates in 1681, his legal career soon prospered, and he rose to become one of the Principal Clerks of Session in 1686. On the proceeds of his legal practice, Mackenzie purchased an estate at King's Cramond near Edinburgh in 1697. In 1705, he followed this with the purchase of the larger property of Delvine in Perthshire. The family continued to prosper for some time and in the early 19th century John Mackenzie's grandson was created Baronet of Delvine.

On 27 April 1691 John Mackenzie received a letter from his friend, Alexander Monro, then a Regent at St Andrews University, informing him that he had despatched to him by bearer 'ane Sett of Golfe-Clubs'.[5]

Like his friend, John Mackenzie, Alexander Monro had also begun his career in the legal profession, in his case as a Writer in Edinburgh. This letter, and the twenty or so others in the collection written by him to John Mackenzie between 1688 and 1697, suggest that they had known each other in Edinburgh legal circles and become firm friends. When he wrote in the spring of 1691 Monro had recently taken up the position of Regent and Professor of Philosophy at St Andrews University. He was to become Provost or Principal of St Salvator's College, St Andrews, before his death in 1697. Monro's business interests and later his academic appointments may have taken him from Edinburgh after 1688, but the letters indicate he was determined not to lose touch with his friends. In a letter of May 1688 he writes, *'I always mynd my friends and sometimes drink their health and particularly yours'.*[6] What better

Letter of Alexander Monro to John Mackenzie of Delvine, 27 April 1691.
Alexander Monro's letter of 1691 to his friend John Mackenzie informed him that he had despatched to him a gift of *'ane Sett of Golfe-Clubs...from this place the metropolis of Golfing'.*
National Library of Scotland, MS 1393, fols 177-8.

4   National Library of Scotland, MSS. 1101-1530. See also W.K. Dickson, 'Letters to John Mackenzie of Delvine, Advocate...1690-1698', in Miscellany of the Scottish History Society, Vol. V (1933), pp. 197-290.
5   National Library of Scotland, MS. 1393, fols 177-8.
6   National Library of Scotland, MS. 1393, fol 170.

way to maintain a friendship than to send a present of a set of golf clubs and balls from '*the metropolis of Golfing*'?

Monro's gift was clearly a present from one golfer to another, although as they had not met for some time he apologised in case the clubs and balls were not suitable. '*I might have made the set to consist of more but I know not your play*'. Three different clubs are mentioned: '*an play club, ane scraper, and ane tin fac'd club*'. Apparently others were available in St Andrews at the time as, Monro acknowledged, they were also in Edinburgh. Golf balls too, were sent by the bearer, and we are told that these could be changed if they proved inappropriate either for Mackenzie's style of play or his chosen course.

The letter indicates that there was a regular traffic in golfing equipment between St Andrews and Edinburgh in the late 17th century. So concerned was Munro about possible confusion with other golfing items carried by the bearer, or indeed theft, that he felt it necessary to advise his friend that the distinguishing marks of the tradesman's and Mackenzie's initials had been stamped on both the clubs and balls.

'Golfers on the Links at St Andrews', c.1680.
This painting by an unknown artist may be the earliest picture to show golf being played in Britain.
Royal and Ancient Golf Club, St Andrews.

FACING PAGE
Letter of James Morice to John Mackenzie, 26 November 1712.
In this letter to his employer James Morice enquires how often his charges are to be allowed to play golf.
National Library of Scotland, MS. 1400, fol. 152.

In addition to correspondence with old and valued friends such as Alexander Monro, John Mackenzie of Delvine's papers include accounts accompanied by reports in the form of a series of letters from James Morice, an employee engaged to help with the upbringing of Mackenzie's large family of fifteen children by his three wives.[7]

James Morice was employed by John Mackenzie between 1707 and 1716 as tutor or governor to three of his sons: Alexander, born in 1695, and the twins Kenneth and Thomas, born in 1699. John Mackenzie's family seems to have been too large to have all lived together in the one house, and when Morice was first employed as tutor the twins were staying with him at Craigie, a village a few miles from Delvine. His pupils were then quite young, and Morice reports '*my Lads have not yet begun as yet to write*'.

Kenneth and Thomas joined their older brother, Alexander, at St Andrews University in 1711, and the letters suggest that James Morice did not accom-

---

7 National Library of Scotland, MS. 1400. For a more detailed discussion of these papers see William Croft Dickinson, *Two Students at St Andrews, 1711-16* (Edinburgh, 1952).

pany them. A letter home from Alexander indicates that this arrangement was not satisfactory as regards the twins' education, as he writes to his father giving a well-worn excuse: '*the true reason that they [Kenneth and Thomas] are so idle is that they are the best scholars in their class*'. By the start of the 1712-13 session James Morice had resumed his charge, overseeing the boys' education, accommodation, and even their recreations.

Their tutor's discipline seems to have had the desired effect, and in September 1713 Kenneth wrote home: '*By being kept close at our studies we find that now to be an easy diversion, which which [sic] was wont to be a fashious [tedious] task*'. Life as a student under James Morice was not all work, and in his first letter from St Andrews to John Mackenzie he enquires '*what you allow on ye young Gentlemen weekly for yr diversion at the golf*'. John Mackenzie is known to have been a golfer himself, and clearly approved of the recreation, and so the answer is hardly surprising: '*When the weather is fair I allow the Twins to go to the golf twice a week according to your order*'. Morice's accounts indicate that the boys took full advantage of this instruction and more as, save when exams loomed, they might be found on the Links as often as three times a week.

The main interest of the accounts lies in the information they give of golfing equipment. Balls and clubs seem to have been purchased locally, and Henry Mills, club-maker in St Andrews, is mentioned by name. Of the three boys, Alexander was probably the best golfer. He had three clubs in his set each costing 12 shillings. The twins at first had one club each worth 10 shillings; later their clubs cost 12 shillings each. This may have been because they became more skilful or merely because they were older. There is a record of the purchase of an iron club for the twins to share which cost one pound and four shillings. Parts of the club might be purchased separately: a club-head cost 4 shillings or 6 shillings, a new shaft 4 shillings, and '*a horn to Thomas's club*' was 2 shillings. On average, clubs lasted about ten rounds, but new balls had to be bought for each game. Balls too came in varying sizes and qualities. Alexander's balls cost 4 shillings each but the twins never progressed beyond the 2 shilling balls.[8]

The annual expenditure for the three boys on golf as recorded by Morice has been calculated as being greater than that for their tuition.[9] Between November 1712 and February 1713, when the boys were playing at least twice a week, Morice spent £17 13 shillings on golfing equipment. Sir John Foulis, who played about once a fortnight on Leith Links in the 1680s, spent £21 on golf in four months in the winter of 1686. As well as clubs and balls, his total bill included expenditure on wagers, coach-hire, and post-match entertainment.[10]

8   The Mackenzie boys' expenses at St Andrews are considered in detail in David Hamilton, *St Andrews Golf* (Glasgow,1986).
9   Hamilton, *St Andrews Golf.*
10   See Chapter 6.

ABOVE
Accounts of James Morice, November 1714.
James Morice's accounts include payments for golfing equipment. *National Library of Scotland, MS. 1400, fol. 253.*

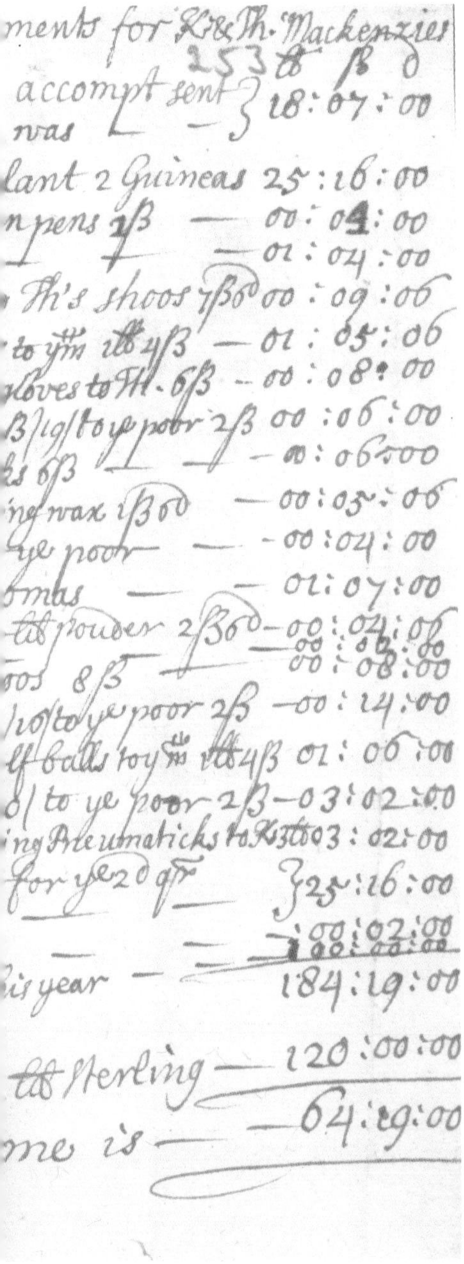

[Handwritten manuscript in left margin, partially legible:]

```
ments for K & Th. Mackenzies
              2538  12  0
accompt sent  18:07:00
was
lant 2 Guineas  25:16:00
n pens 2/3  —  00:04:00
           —  01:04:00
Th's shoos 7/6  00:09:06
to ythm ilk 4/3  —  01:05:06
loves to Th. 6/3  —  00:08:00
3/19/to ye poor 2/3  00:06:00
ts 6/3  —  00:06:00
ing wax 1/3  —  00:03:06
ye poor  —  00:04:00
omas  —  01:07:00
tt pouder 2/3  00-00:02:06
                  00:08:00
oos 8/3
/19/to ye poor 2/3  —  00:14:00
lf balls to ythm ilk 4/3  01:06:00
d/ to ye poor 2/3 — 03:02:00
ing Pneumaticks to K 3tt  03:02:00
for ye 20 qr  25:16:00
              00:02:00
              00:02:00
is year  —  184:19:00
tt Sterling  —  120:00:00
me is  —  64:19:00
```

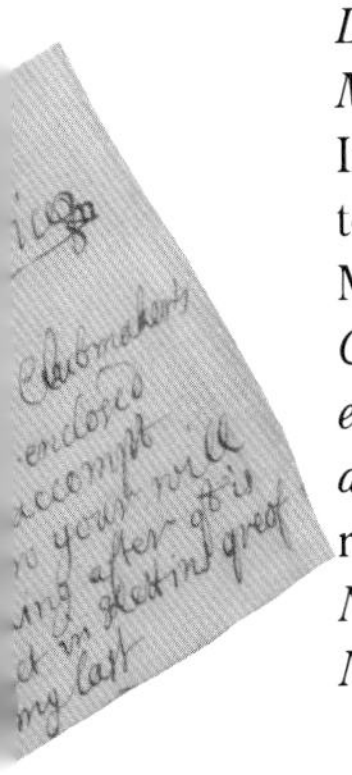

1714
Accompt of Disbursements for K[enneth] and Th[omas] Mackenzies

	£ sh d
Ballance of the last year's accompt sent	
over Novr. 1714 due to me was	18:07:00
1 Nov. to yr [their] Regent Mr. Vilant 2 Guineas	25:16:00
7 to ye poor 2sh /8/ for 2 dozen pens 2sh	00:04:00
11 for an iron club to ythm [them]	01:04:00
14 to the poor 2sh /17/ for soling Th[omas]'s shoos 7sh 6d	00:09:06
21 to ye poor 2sh 6d /25/ for 13 balls to ythm [them] ilk 4sh 3d	01:05:06

Alexander left University in 1713 and became a lawyer, being admitted a Writer to the Signet in 1714. In 1718, he followed his father as one of the Principal Clerks of Session, succeeding to Delvine in 1731. Of the twins, Kenneth left St Andrews in 1716 and continued his studies at Leyden. He returned to Scotland and was admitted to the Faculty of Advocates in 1718. He became Professor of Civil Law at Edinburgh University and died in 1756. Thomas's fate was not so happy. The letters suggest that he was sickly with a recurring cough. He died in 1720, possibly from pulmonary consumption, only four years after he graduated.

James Melville's diary showed golf was played by students at St Andrews in 1574, and Bishop Hamilton's Acknowledgement indicated the game was popular at least as early as 1552 (see Chapter 3). In 1642, sport was sanctioned at St Andrews University by a report of the University Commissioners which stated that '*Recreations are necessary*'. The Report went on to state that only '*laufull exercises, as gouffe, archery, and other of that kind, which are harmeles and do exercise the body*' were permitted, and specifically decreed '*there be no carding, dyceing, amongst the students, or exercises of that kynd*'.[11]

The Delvine papers indicate that in the early 18th century, as in the time of James Melville over a hundred years before, golf was popular at St Andrews with both students and staff. Alexander Monro's letter of 1691 shows that even senior academics indulged, and in 1713 Morice relates how '*since the days become longer, the Masters of the University are found out at the golf in the afternoon*'. John Mackenzie sanctioned the quite considerable expenditure on golf gladly, and from the importance he attached to the game it would seem he considered it to be no mere recreation but an accomplishment which would stand his sons in good stead throughout their professional lives.

Letter of James Morice to John Mackenzie, 2 June 1713.
In a postscript to this letter to his employer, James Morice notes '*Henry Mill ye Clubmaker's receipt is herein enclosed together wit ye accompt...*' Unfortunately, the receipt has not survived.
National Library of Scotland, MS. 1400, fol. 167.

11 St Andrews University Commissioners' Reports, 206.

Thro' flow'ry Vallies, and enamel'd Meads,
The hastening Flood at length to Glasgow speeds
Its Northern Bank a lovely Green displays,
Whose e'ery Prospect fresh Delights conveys.

THE Muse would sing, when Glasgow she surveys,
But Glasgow's Beauty shall outlast her lays.
Tho' small in Compass, not the lest in Fame,
She boasts her lofty Tow'rs, and antient Name.

Extract from James Arbuckle
Glotta (Glasgow, 1721).
National Library of Scotland.

9 'GLOTTA'

AN EYE-WITNESS ACCOUNT, GLASGOW, 1721

J. Brooks, 'The Glasgow Bridges and Merchants Tower', 1806.
This watercolour painting depicts some of the numerous activities which took place on Glasgow Green: children play, dogs frisk, and the gentry stroll, while close at hand milkmaids and washer-women toil.
People's Palace (Glasgow Museums).

ALTHOUGH MOST EARLY SCOTTISH GOLF TOOK PLACE ON THE EAST COAST, THE game was known in Glasgow from at least 1589, when the Kirk Session issued a fierce lambast against ball and stick games, decreeing that there be '*no golf, carrict, [or] shinnie [variants of shinty] in the High or the Blackfriars Yards, Sunday or weekday*'.[1] In banning these games entirely from certain areas, the Church in Glasgow took a different attitude towards golf from that of most other Kirk Sessions: parish records elsewhere, from Perth and Stirling to Banff and Cullen, were generally concerned with Sunday observance and forbade golf on the Sabbath or merely '*in tyme of sermonis*' (see Chapter 1). Given that the game in the street must have been extremely dangerous and a nuisance to passers-by, Glasgow Kirk Session's decree shows a commendable concern for public safety.

The then relatively small town of Glasgow had no coastal links for the recreation of its citizens, and the area of common land on the north bank of the Clyde known as Glasgow Green was popular for outdoor activities. The Green has had a variety of functions over the centuries: horses and cattle have grazed there during the summer months; crops of grass were grown for sale; there were also orchards, and vegetable gardens, and flower beds laid out between paths and trees made it a pleasant place to stroll. In addition, the Green was popular for games and pastimes, one of which was golf. The records of Glasgow Golf Club indicate they played on the Green from at least 1787 when their surviving minute books start.

While the accounts of the Earls of Annandale record payments for golf clubs and balls for the young Earl William and his brother while at Glasgow Grammar School in 1674,[2] it is impossible to estimate how much golf was played in 17th-century Glasgow. In 1642, however, Glasgow University, like St Andrews University in the same year, gave its approval to the game when it pronounced that '*the scholars be excerised in lawful games such as Gouffe, Archerie, and the lyk*'.[3] It seems probable that the students took advantage of

[1] James Colville, *The Glasgow Golf Club* (Glasgow, 1907), p. 1.
[2] Sir William Fraser, *The Annandale Family Book of the Johnstones, Earls and Marquises of Annandale* (Edinburgh, 1894), p. ccliii.
[3] Maitland Club, 72 (Glasgow, 1854), Vol. 2, p. 466.

this excuse to escape from their studies, and in 1721 one of them wrote what may well be the earliest surviving eye-witness account of a game of golf in Scotland.

Little is known about James Arbuckle: he is thought to have been born in Ireland in 1700, and was a friend of the poet Allan Ramsay who himself alluded to golf in his poems, 'Health', and 'Elegy on the Death of Maggy Johnston' (see Chapter 7). By the time *Glotta* was published in 1721 Arbuckle had already had some limited success as a poet, but it is for *Glotta* he is chiefly known. The poem gives a detailed description of the course of the River Clyde (the 'Glotta' of the title), and doing so, records a game of golf on Glasgow Green.[4]

James Arbuckle, Glotta *(Glasgow, 1721).* In his poem eulogising the River Clyde, James Arbuckle records a game of golf on Glasgow Green. *National Library of Scotland.*

The hastening Flood at length to Glasgow *speeds.*
Its Northern *Bank a lovely Green displays,*
Whose e'ery Prospect fresh Delights conveys.

In Winter *too, when hoary Frosts o'erspread,*
The verdant Turf, and naked lay the Mead,
The vig'rous Youth commence the sportive War,
And arm'd with Lead, their jointed Clubs prepare;
The Timber Curve to Leathern Orbs apply,
Compact, Elastic, to pervade the Sky:
These to the distant Hole direct they drive;
They claim the Stakes who thither first arrive.
Intent his Ball the eager Gamester eyes,
His Muscles strains, and various Postures tries,
Th' impelling Blow to strike with greater Force,
And shape the motive Orb's projectile Course.
If with due Strength the weighty Engine fall,
Discharg'd obliquely, and impinge the Ball,
It winding mounts aloft, and sings in Air;
And wond'ring Crowds the Gamester's Skill declare.
But when some luckless wayward Stroke descends,
Whose Force the Ball in running quickly spends,
The Foes triumph, the Club is curs'd in vain;
Spectators scoff, and ev'n Allies complain.
Thus still Success is follow'd with Applause;
But ah! how few espouse a vanquish'd Cause!

GLOTTA

A

POEM

Humbly infcribed to the Right Honourable the
MARQUESS of CARNARVON.

By Mr. ARBUCKLE, Student in the
Univerfity of GLASGOW.

Tu mihi, Timoleon, magni fpes maxima Patris,
Nec Patriæ minor, Aonii novus incola Montis,
Adde gradum comes. ———— Buch: de Sphæra.

GLASGOW,
Printed by WILLIAM DUNCAN, and are to be fold in his Shop in the *Salt-Mercat.*
M. DCC. XXI.

Only a short section of *Glotta* is devoted to Glasgow Green, which Arbuckle describes as an area of land given over to recreation, '*Whose e'ery Prospect fresh Delights conveys*'. According to the poem, the Green was popular for an evening stroll — '*Here, when declining Sol extends the shades, Resort victorious Throngs of charming Maids*'. Arbuckle adds to the picturesque scene by informing the reader that the young ladies were dressed in plaids.

---

[4] For a more detailed discussion of James Arbuckle's *Glotta* see David Hamilton, *Early Golf in Glasgow, 1587-1787* (Oxford, 1985).

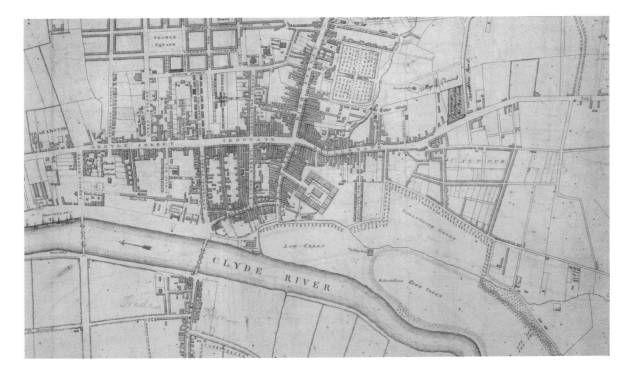

'Plan of the City of Glasgow, Board of Ordnance, 1792'.
This late 18th-century plan of Glasgow, made for the Board of Ordnance, shows the Low Green and High Green alongside the River Clyde. The Washing House, the Herds' House and the Slaughter House are all marked.
National Library of Scotland, Z2/79a.

Others have given a less romanticised picture of Glasgow Green at the time. James Colville, writing in *The Glasgow Golf Club*, 1907, bemoans the conditions in Arbuckle's time. On his Green, golfers would have had to contend with *'the daily accumulating filth washed down to the Clyde from the Gallowgate, the skinners' yards, redolent of tan, tripe, tallow, and tharm [gut]'*. The area was also liable to flooding, leading to deep cart tracks which must have led to many an erratic bounce.

But this is to detract from Arbuckle's scene. Into his idyllic gathering he introduces a group of winter golfers, and then *'The vig'rous Youth commence the sportive War'*. We are not told who the players were, and are left to speculate as to whether they were Arbuckle's fellow students at the University. Arbuckle then proceeds to describe the players' expensive golfing equipment consisting of lead, *'jointed'*, clubs and *'Compact, Elastic'*, leather (probably featherie) balls, in what must have been a game between quite wealthy players. This was a game of match-play rather than stroke-play, and *'Allies'* are mentioned, indicating a foursome.

David Hamilton suggests that James Arbuckle was not a golfer himself, as he seems to consider the game to be one of strength rather than timing, and states that the first player to reach the hole would win the *'stakes'*. Perhaps Arbuckle identified more with the excited crowd of clearly knowledgeable spectators than with the players. Be that as it may, his poem has provided us with an important, detailed, account of the way golf was played in the early 18th century.

Goff, and the Man, I sing, who, em'lous,[1] plies,
The jointed club; whose balls invade the skies;
Who from Edina's [Edinburgh's] tow'rs, his peaceful home,
In quest of fame o'er Letha's [Leith's] plains did roam.
Long toil'd the hero, on the verdant field,
Strain'd his stout arm the weighty club to wield;
Such toils it cost, such labours to obtain
The bays of conquest, and the bowl to gain.

O thou GOLFINIA, Goddess of these plains,
Great Patroness of GOFF, indulge my strains;
Whether beneath the thorn-tree shade you lie,
Or from Mercerian tow'rs the game survey,
Or, round the green the flying ball you chase,
Or make your bed in some hot sandy face:
Leave your much lov'd abode, inspire his lays
Who sings of GOFF, and sings thy fav'rit's praise.

North from Edina eight furlongs and more,
Lies that fam'd field, on Fortha's sounding shore.
Here, Caledonian Chiefs for health resort,
Confirm their sinews by the manly sport.

[1]   Emulous, i.e. in a spirit of eager rivalry.

10 'THE GOFF'

EDINBURGH, 1743

THOMAS MATHISON'S MOCK-HEROIC EPIC POEM *THE GOFF*, PUBLISHED IN Edinburgh in 1743, is almost certainly the first printed book devoted entirely to golf. The author was born in 1720, the son of an Edinburgh merchant. As a young man he worked as a lawyer in the city, but his career changed direction when he was ordained in 1750. He was appointed Minister of Brechin in 1754 where he remained until his early death in 1760 some six years later. Although he is not known to have written anything else on golf, this poem seems to have arisen out of his love of the game. As a keen golfer, he was almost certainly a member of the Company of Gentlemen Golfers, later the Honourable Company of Edinburgh Golfers, one of the earliest Golf Clubs.

The Goff is a poem in three cantos, each over a hundred lines in length, which tells of a game of golf played on Leith Links. These Links, where Sir John Foulis and Thomas Kincaid played in the 1680s, are glowingly described as '*that fam'd field, on* Fortha's *sounding shore. / Here* Caledonian *Chiefs for health resort, / Confirm their sinews by the manly sport*'. The first edition, shown here, and the second edition of 1763, give only the initials of the 'Caledonian *Chiefs*', and the implication is that these were important figures in Edinburgh society needing no further identification to their contemporaries. The third edition, published in 1793, gives the names in full.

The poem lists the following golfers: '*Macdonald and unmatc'd Dalrymple ply/ Their pond'rous weapons, and the green defy; / Rattray for skill, and Corse for strength renown'd, / Stewart and Lesly beat the sandy ground, And Brown and Alston, Chiefs well known to fame, / And numbers more the Muse forbears to name*'. Most of these players, many of whom were celebrated lawyers and judges, are known to have been among the first members of the Company of Gentlemen Golfers. Among those named are Lord President Forbes, Lord Drummore, and Sir Alexander Macdonald. Although the poem shows that these golfers knew each other well and played together regularly, there is no indication that they belonged to a Golf Club at the time of the poem.

Lord President Forbes was an eminent Scottish lawyer and politician described in the anonymous pamphlet *Memoirs of Duncan Forbes of Culloden*, (probably published in 1748), as '*a man of such abilities, as would have enabled him to make a bright figure in any station of life*'.[2] In spite of the burdens of

2   Anon, *Memoirs of Duncan Forbes of Culloden* (Edinburgh, c.1748).

FACING PAGE LEFT
Jamison, 'Duncan Forbes of Culloden'.
Scottish National Portrait Gallery.

FACING PAGE RIGHT AND BELOW
Thomas Mathison, The Goff: An Heroi-Comical Poem (Edinburgh, 1743).
National Library of Scotland.

work, Duncan Forbes's *Memoirs* indicate his legal duties do not seem to have prevented from him playing a regular round of golf.

While Lord Advocate, the *Memoirs* relate that '*during the time of the summer session at Edinburgh, [Forbes] went out every Saturday to Stonie-hill, and ...except the time he devoted to hearing sermon, tasted the pleasures of a country life till the Monday that he came to Leith, and there played at the golf*'. Forbes also played at Musselburgh. In 1728 he wrote to his brother from Stoneyhill '*This Day after a Very hard Pull I Got the better of My Son at the Gouf in Musselburgh Links, if he was as Good at any Other thing as he is at that there might be some hopes of him*'.

Later, when deeply embroiled in the aftermath of the Jacobite Rising of 1745, Forbes had less time for golf and in 1746 was to lament this in a letter to his cousin, William Forbes: '*I long to hear what has become of all my golf companions, particularly whether John Rattray is come back...for I have not for these five months seen anyone that could give me the least satisfaction to my anxiety to know*'. The loss of his regular game must have been particularly galling as Forbes had been first recorded Captain of the Company of Gentlemen Golfers in 1744. The John Rattray enquired about by Forbes was the '*Surgeon Rattray*' of *The Goff*. He won Edinburgh's competition for the Silver Club in 1744 and 1745. Rattray was a supporter of the Jacobite cause, becoming personal physician to Prince Charles Edward Stuart: he was taken prisoner at Culloden, and was released on the intervention of his friend Duncan Forbes.

To return to *The Goff*, having set the scene on Leith Links, Mathison then introduces his main protagonists: two keen young golfers, identified in the poem only as '*Castalio*' and '*Pygmalion*'. He writes: '*Bright Phoebus now, had measur'd half the day / And warm'd the earth with genial noon-tide ray: / Forth rush'd Castalio and his daring foe, / Both arm'd with clubs, and eager for the blow*'.[3]

The two players were accompanied by '*tattered Irus, who their armour bears*'. He acted as caddy to them both and also prepared their tees. Mathison records that he '*Upon the green two little pyr'mids rears; / On these they place two balls with careful eye*'. His duties at the tee performed, Irus seems to have gone on ahead to mark where the balls landed. In the days of unprepared courses, a fore-caddy was probably much in demand.

The poem records in some detail the progress of the match at all of the five named holes of the course at Leith: the Thorn-tree hole, the Braehead hole, the Sawmill hole, the North Mid-hole, and the South Mid-hole. A match might have consisted of two, three, four, or even five rounds of the course. In this

An intriguing record of Duncan Forbes's game has survived in the *Memoirs*: *He discoverd a dissatisfaction with such as played carelessly, and never seemed better pleased than when his antagonists exerted themselves against him. He struck the ball full, and having a nervous arm upon a well-pois'd body, he generally drove very far; when nigh the hole, he tipped with so much caution and circumspection that even a lesson might be learned from him in his innocent amusements.*

BELOW
Tableau depicting Allan Robertson stuffing a golf ball, c.1840.
Allan Robertson (1815-59) was the son of a St Andrews golf ball-maker, and the outstanding golfer of his generation.
British Golf Museum, St Andrews.

---

[3]   C.B. Clapcott, in his commentary on *The Goff* (National Library of Scotland MS. 3999), has identified '*Castilio*' as Alexander Dunning, an Edinburgh bookseller, and '*Pygmalion*', the loser of the match, as the author, Thomas Mathison himself.

ABOVE

Letter of Duncan Forbes to his brother, John Forbes of Culloden, 1728.
In his letter to his brother, Duncan Forbes tells of a golfing expedition to Musselburgh Links.
National Library of Scotland, MS. 2967, fol. 98v.

case, there were four rounds, and twenty holes were played. The match had been started under the noon-time sun, but by the time the last hole, which decided the match, was reached, '*Declining* Sol *with milder beams invades / The* Scotian *fields, and lengthens out the shades*'.

Golf courses of the time, and indeed much later, did not have a set number of holes and usually had far fewer than today's standard eighteen, the exception being St Andrews where there were twenty-two holes when the Royal and Ancient was formed. The course was shortened in 1750 to twenty holes. Later, it was reduced to eighteen.

As in James Arbuckle's description of Glasgow golf in his *Glotta* of 1721, the equipment is expensive. Clubs are said to be '*jointed*' and the balls are featheries. Mathison gives a graphic description of the making of a featherie ball. They are '*The work of* Bobson; *who with matchless art / Shapes the firm hide, connecting ev'ry part...And thro' the eylet drives the downy tide; / Crowds urging crowds the forceful brogue impels, / The feathers harden and the leather swells;/ He crams and sweats, yet crams and urges more, / Til scarce the turgid globe contains its store*'. It is interesting to note that Bobson, probably a contraction of 'Robertson', was a St Andrews ball-maker, and the implication is that although golf balls were made in Leith at the time, the most prized balls came from St Andrews.

We are told less about the making of the clubs used for the match than the balls. Reference is made to Andrew Dickson of Leith, one of the leading club-makers of the time: '*Of finest ash* Castalio's *shaft was made / Pond'rous with lead and fenc'd with horn the head, / The work of* Dickson *who in* Letha *dwells / (And in the art of making clubs excels)*'. Shafts were probably made from ash although hickory was not unknown in Britain in the early 18th century. Thomas Kincaid, writing in 1687, stated that the shafts should be of hazel. We are not told how many clubs the players had with them, but it seems likely that Castilio had only one iron club.

There is some evidence that Scottish golfing equipment was highly regarded abroad and was exported from the 17th century (see p. 25). The Scots might have imported golf balls from Low Countries from the 1490s, but in turn Dutch golfers might buy their clubs from Scotland. American Manor Court records indicate that Dutch settlers were playing golf around the present city of Albany, New York, in 1650.[4] The earliest reference to the export of golfing equipment to America is in the Port of Leith Customs Account Books for 1743 when eight dozen golf clubs and three gross (432) golf balls were shipped in the *Magdalen* to David Deas of South Carolina.[5] Customs account books for Greenock in 1750 and Glasgow in 1765 show similar exports.

[4]   van Hengel, p. 66.
[5]   Scottish Record Office, E5/22/1.

Further evidence of international trade in golfing equipment in the 17th century was uncovered in the 1970s when the wreck of the Dutch East Indiaman, the *Kennemerland*, shipwrecked off the Outer Skerries, Shetland, in 1664, was excavated. Among the pewter bottle tops, clay pipes, and lead shot, were five objects now identified as golf club heads. The heads consist of a central wooden core around which there is a lead alloy shell. The best preserved head is marked with a group of parallel lines and crosses. These may have been purely decorative, but seem more likely to include the stamps of the club-maker and of the city in which they were made. The clubs were new when they were put on board the ship, and were probably carried for trading purposes rather than being part of the luggage of an individual. Interestingly, three of the clubs were intended for left-handed play.[6]

As might be expected, in addition to exporting golfing equipment, when Scots golfers left their own country they took their game with them. One such was Alexander Carlyle. Born in 1722, Carlyle was the son of the Minister of Prestonpans in East Lothian. After graduating from Edinburgh University he studied at Glasgow and Leyden Universities before being ordained Minister of Inveresk, Musselburgh, in 1748. Carlyle was friendly with many of the leading literary figures of the day and a keen supporter of the arts. His 'Autobiography' gives the impression of a genial, cultured, and liberal man.[7] Unfortunately, his love of the theatre led him to fall foul of the Church establishment. Carlyle made several transcripts of *Douglas*, a play by his friend John Hume, and attended rehearsals and even a performance. For this he was censured by the Synod of Lothian and Tweeddale. Nevertheless, he remained Minister of Inveresk until his death in 1805.

While in London for his sister's wedding in 1758, Carlyle regularly met his Scottish friends, including John Hume, William Robertson the historian, and the architects Robert and James Adam, for theatre visits followed by dinner. On one occasion, the friends were invited to the house of David Garrick the actor, for dinner at his Hampton villa and a round of golf.

Unfortunately, there is no description of the actual game. After they had played, the party went on to Garrick's villa where they met with Mrs Garrick '*a woman of uncommon good sense*'. While the company waited in the garden for dinner, Carlyle showed off his golfing skills and records his prowess with a notable lack of modesty:

> *Having Observed a Green Mound in the Garden opposite the archway, I said to our Landlord, that While the Servants were preparing the Colla-*

Reproductions of clubs such as may have been exported from Leith to South Carolina aboard the 'Magdalen' in 1743.
This set of reproduction clubs includes a play club, a long spoon, a short spoon, a putter, a heavy square toe iron, and a light 'driving' iron.
Oscroft Golf.

Port of Leith Custom Collector's Quarterly Account Book, 1743.
Eight dozen golf clubs and three gross golf balls (432) were exported from Leith to South Carolina aboard the *Magdalen* in 1743.
Scottish Record Office, E5/22/1.

6   C.T.C. Dobbs, and R.A.Price, 'The Kennemerland site. An Interim Report. The sixth and seventh seasons, 1982 and 1987, and the identification of five golf clubs', in *The International Journal of Nautical Archaeology*, Vol. 20, no. 2 (May 1991), pp. 110-122.
7   Alexander Carlyle's 'Autobiography', National Library of Scotland, MSS. 23911-16. See *The Autobiography of...Dr. Alexander Carlyle, Minister of Inveresk*, edited by John Hill Burton (Edinburgh, 1860).

Henry Raeburn,
'Alexander Carlyle'.
Scottish National Portrait
Gallery.

He had told us to bring Golph
Clubs and Balls, that we
might play at that Game on
Molesly Hurst. As we pasd
thro' Kensignton [sic] the
Coldstream Regt. were
changing Guard, and seeing
our Clubs they gave us 3
cheers in Honour of a
Diversion peculiar to Scotland ...we cross'd the River to
the Golphing Ground w[hich]
was very Good. None of the
Company could play but J.
Home and myself and Parson
Black from Aberdeen.[8]

Alexander Carlyle from Hugh
Paton, Original Portraits ...by
the late John Kay...
(Edinburgh, 1842).

tion in the Temple I would surprise him with a stroke at the Golph, as I
should Drive a Ball thro' his archway into the Thames, once in three
strokes. I had measured the Distance with my Eye in walking about the
Garden, and accordingly at the 2nd stroke made the Ball alight in the
Mouth of the Gateway, and Roll down the Green Slope into the River. This
was so Dextrous that he was quite surprised, and beg'd the Club of me, by
Which such a Feat had been perform'd.[8]

Living close to Musselburgh Links as Minister of Inveresk for over fifty years,
it is hardly surprising Carlyle was a golfer. Interestingly, he informs us other
Scots in the party including Robert and James Adam did not know how to play.
The implication in the 'Autobiography' is that, in the mid-18th century, golf in
England was still considered to be a Scottish rather than an English game.

Sir John Foulis's accounts mention a *company* of golfers playing on Leith
Links in the 1680s (Chapter 6), and the origins of the Golf Clubs probably lie
in such informal gatherings. It is difficult to be precise about the date of
founding of individual Clubs due to lack of documentary evidence, but it was
in the 1740s that the earliest Clubs were established and the process began
of transforming what had been a largely informal game into a highly
organised sport.

[8]   Alexander Carlyle's 'Autobiography', National Library of Scotland, MS. 23915.

The Rules of the Company of Gentlemen Golfers, later the Honourable Company of Edinburgh Golfers, date from 1744, while the code of the Society of St Andrews Golfers, now the Royal and Ancient Golf Club in St Andrews, appears in their earliest minute book dated 1754. Other Clubs, too, were formed about this time. The Edinburgh (later Royal) Burgess Golfing Society was clearly well-established by 1774 when its earliest surviving minute book starts but a foundation date of 1735 is claimed; the Royal Musselburgh Golf Club was founded in 1774 but there is no documentary evidence until 1784; and the Bruntsfield Golf Club claims a foundation date of 1761, but their first list of members and minute book date from 1787.

In their history of Royal Blackheath Golf Club, Henderson and Stirk suggest that the earliest Scottish Golfing Societies may have been formed by groups of freemasons who took up the game as a healthy form of exercise prior to their feasting and masonic rituals.[9] Their devotion to golf may well have kept the game alive in Scotland at the time when it virtually died out in the Low Countries. Henderson and Stirk go on to suggest that the almost universal lack of evidence to document the early days of the Clubs is no coincidence, and that the minutes and other records were systematically destroyed in an attempt to hide the game's masonic origins in the mid-18th century when non-masons began to be admitted to the Clubs in significant numbers. Perhaps masonic involvement may go some way to explain the lack of female participation in the game of golf, not to mention other sports.

The 18th-century Golfing Societies were very much the preserve of wealthy merchants, landowners, academics, and professional men, who saw golf as a means to display status, wealth, and achievement, as well as a pleasant recreation: there can be no doubt that the Clubs were socially exclusive. By their very nature most of the personal records that survive to this day — be they letters, diaries, or account books — are papers of the wealthier members of society. Golfing equipment was expensive, and from the time of the emergence of the featherie ball in the early 17th-century must have been beyond the pocket of the average craftsman or labourer. Golf had previously been played without expensively crafted clubs or hand-stitched balls and there is evidence in the records of the Town Councils, the Incorporations, and the Kirk Sessions, that it continued to be enjoyed by men and women from a wide range of social backgrounds. However, by the mid-18th century Golfing Societies were proliferating in Scotland, and with their emergence the nature of the sport changed. The rules and regulations, competitions, and formal social activities which developed with the Clubs took the game into another era, and were to make golf the game we know today.

---

[9]   Ian T. Henderson and David I. Stirk, *Royal Blackheath Golf Club* (London, 1981).